*Dedicated to all lovers
of Indian food who provide me
with the inspiration
and encouragement to keep
experimenting. May that tribe
increase and make Indian food the
most popular in the world.*

Simply Indian

Simply Indian

SANJEEV KAPOOR

IN ASSOCIATION WITH ALYONA KAPOOR

PopulaR
prakashan

Popular Prakashan Pvt. Ltd.
35-C, Pt Madan Mahon Malaviya Marg
Tardeo, Mumbai 400 034.

First Publication 2003
First Reprint December 2003

(3861)

ISBN-81-7991-115-2

Book Design : Gopi Kukde
Photography : Mangesh Parab
Food Stylist : Harpal Singh Sokhi

Typeset
at Vans Information Ltd.
35-C, Pt Madan Mohan Malaviya Marg
Tardeo, Mumbai 400 034.

Printed In India
by Vakil & Sons Pvt. Ltd., Industry Manor, 2nd Floor, Worli,
Mumbai and Published by Ramdas Bhatkal
for Popular Prakashan Pvt. Ltd.
35-C, Pandit Madan Mohan Malaviya Marg
Tardeo, Mumbai 400 034.

If the question is 'Why another book on Indian Cuisine?' The answer is 'Why Not!' It's my passion, it's my niche, it's loved globally and it's to be glorified till eternity. Indian Cuisine deserves as much attention as it can get from all quarters of the world.

Indian food is simple yet it has a rich history. It has a lavish cultural background what with the *rajahs* and *maharajahs* of eons past having a fired up enthusiasm for delectable preparations. Food flourished in those days with the royal chefs vying with each other to create exotic delicacies for their monarchs. We are enjoying the fruits of that labour as hundreds of years of patronage to the joy and art of cooking has given us an inexhaustible record of delicious recipes.

Moreover who can overlook the influence of vegetarianism that has deep-rooted origins in India? The world is turning vegetarian gradually and it is Indian food to a considerable extent which has resulted in this trend. Vegetarianism in India has been influenced mainly by the Indian prince and founder of Buddhism, Lord Buddha; founder of Jainism, Lord Mahavir and King Ashoka. Our food is gaining in popularity because it has a lot of fascinating flavours, is healthy and easy to digest. People who are becoming conscious about food intake, especially fat intake, are looking for taste, appearance and variety in the foods that they eat. Indian food is the answer because of its uniqueness, its strong flavours and interesting textures. It is a delightful presentation of spices, seasonings, leafy vegetables, grains, meats, fruits and legumes.

One must realise that Indian food is what it is now through a process of evolution! The recipes have been passed from generation to generation, from mother to daughter and the present generation is dependent on such records as also good cookbooks and web-sites with some great recipes. This is an exciting era as the awareness about health is widespread. Indian cuisine plays its role to the hilt with its balance of carbohydrates, proteins, fats and micro-nutrients from fruits and vegetables. The health promoting properties of various herbs and spices ensure that all six sensations of taste, sweet, sour, salty, bitter, pungent and astringent are satisfied individually as well as collectively.

India is a large country with a greater diversity of people, language, climate, cultures and religion than almost any other country in the world. We have North Indian cuisine, South Indian Cuisine, Cuisine from the East and Cuisine from the West. We have already talked about the influence of cultures such as Buddhism and Jainism. Indian food is also influenced

Author's Note

by the Aryan settlers, Arab and Chinese traders and the conquerors such as Persians, Mongols, Turks, the British and the Portuguese. Then we also cannot overlook India's ancient science system of the Ayurveda. Ayurveda has given us a comprehensive system of health, diet and nutrition and it is the common thread that runs through all the sub-cultures and regions of our vast country. Indian cuisine is a deep, melting pot with food that is nutritious, beautifully presented and created exquisitely. The recipes given here are samples of foods prepared in different states of the country. You can prepare a Goan 'Chicken Cafreal' or 'Malvani Mutton'. Make a 'Tamatar Chatni' with 'Varqi Parantha' or sip some 'Pepper Rasam'. Wind up with a 'Kesar Pista Kulfi'…and there's so much more.

We should also make a brief mention, in passing, of the Indian Restaurant Cuisine (as opposed to Home Food). Though greatly influenced by North Indian cuisine, many Indian restaurants around the globe are serving Indian food prepared by Indian chefs who have had their culinary training in a foreign country. The result is a blend of two great cuisines! Back home, all restaurant food has become somewhat commercialised. That is why I have been propounding the message of having 'ghar ka khana'.

As I see it, since Indian food is my niche, why not give some personal contribution to this big, impersonal world? I believe that the driving force behind any significant success is the belief that what you are doing is of real consequence. To me, Indian food is Number One in the world and it's a matter of time when the whole wide world will nod its head in agreement. And that will be soon, I'm confident. My goal will be easy to attain because as I understand success is not related to experience, talent, looks, good fortune or inside connections. Success comes from deep passion and total dedication to what you are doing and also having the conviction that what you are doing matters.

I have also been a great fan of Indian food because this cuisine saves time. Many items can be cooked on 'dum', in a pressure cooker or in pans. Beans can be soaked overnight. The dough for 'rotis', 'chapatis' can be kneaded ahead of time and refrigerated. In fact give or take a few minutes, a full Indian Menu can be put onto the table in thirty minutes flat! This is because Indian food is traditionally cooked with feeling rather than with recipes. It is wholesome and extremely easy to prepare. In this collection of delicious Indian food, all recipes serve four people when they are combined with other complementary dishes to form a balanced menu. The following pages hold a veritable treasure of authentic Indian recipes that not only flatter the taste buds but also add a chapter of healthful eating in our lives. Go ahead and enjoy! That's what life is meant for!

Be Indian, Taste Indian, Enjoy Indian. "Simply Indian".

Acknowledgements

A. I. Kazi

Afsheen Panjwani

Anand Bhandiwad

Anil Bhandari

Mrs. Lata Lohana & Capt. K. K. Lohana

Drs. Meena & Ram Prabhoo

Ganesh Pednekar

Gopi Kukde

Grain of Salt, Kolkata

Harpal Singh Sokhi

Hotel Vallerina

Jaideep Chaubal

Jijesh Gangadharan

Jyotsna & Mayur Dvivedi

Lohana Khaandaan

Namita Pusalkar

Namrata & Sanjiv Bahl

Neelima Acharya

Neena Murdeshwar

Pooja & Rajeev Kapoor

Rajeev Matta

Rutika Samtani

Sanjay Ranade

Satish Parab

Shivani Ganesh

Smeeta Bhatkal

Sunit Purandare

Swapna Shinde

The Yellow Chilli, Amritsar

The Yellow Chilli, Jalandhar

The Yellow Chilli, Ludhiana

The Yellow Chilli, Noida

The Yellow Chilli, Pitampura, Delhi

Tripta Bhagattjee

Vinayak Gawande

Ingredient	Measure	Weight
Almonds	10-12	12 gms
Asafoetida powder (hing)	1/2 tsp	5 gms
Baking powder	1 tsp	3 gms
Black gram (urad dhuli), split	1 cup	220 gms
Black pepper powder	1 tsp	3 gms
Butter	1 tbsp	12 gms
Cashewnuts	10-12	7 gms
Cashewnuts paste	1 cup	140 gms
Chopped coriander leaves	1 cup	55 gms
Cloves	20	1 gm
Coriander (dhania) powder	1 tsp	2 gms
	1 tbsp	6 gms
Cumin (jeera) powder	1 tsp	2 gms
	1 tbsp	6 gms
Egg	1	63 gms
Flour (atta)	1 cup	115 gms
Fresh cream	1 cup	250 mls
	1 tbsp	15 mls
Garam masala powder	1 tsp	2 gms
Garlic	6-8 cloves	5 gms
Garlic paste	1 tbsp	16 gms
Ghee	1 tbsp	7 gms
Ginger	1 inch	15-20 gms
Ginger paste	1 tbsp	16 gms
Gramflour (besan)	1 tbsp	10 gms
Grated cheese	1 cup	75 gms
Grated coconut	1 cup	175 gms
Green chillies	10	24 gms
	5	11 gms
Green coriander leaves	1 cup	35 gms
Green peas (frozen)	1 cup	110 gms
Honey	1 tbsp	20 gms
Lemon juice	(1/2 lemon) large sized 1 tsp	3 mls
Mawa (khoya)	1 cup	200 gms
Medium sized carrot	1	60 gms
Medium sized carrot	1	90 gms
Medium sized potato	1	100 gms
Medium sized tomato	1	100 gms
Mustard (rai) powder	1 tsp	2 gms
Oil	1 tbsp	13 mls
Pigeon Pea, split (tooar dal)	1 cup	225 gms
Red chilli (mirch) powder	1 tsp	2 gms
	1 tbsp	5 gms
Refined flour (maida)	1 tbsp	8 gms
	1 cup	200 gms
Rice	1 cup	200 gms
Rice flour	1 tsp	3 gms
	1 tbsp	7 gms
	1 cup	115 gms
Salt	1 tsp	6 gms
Sugar	1 tbsp	14 gms
Tamarind pulp	1 tsp	6 gms

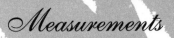

Measurements

Soups, Salads and Starters

Pepper Rasam 15

Palak Shorba 16

Lemon and Coriander Soup 17

Tomato and Paneer Soup 18

Chicken Coconut Rasam 19

Paya Shorba 20

Moong Mauth Chaat 21

Gajar aur Kishmish ka Salad 22

Murgh Shahjahani Chaat 23

Bhutte ke Cutlet 24

Khasta Kachori 27

Hariyali Paneer 28

Vegetable Vermicelli Upma 29

Crunchy Paneer Pakora 30

Kathiawadi Vada 31

Saunfia Paneer Tikka 32

Papad Rolls 33

Kalimirch Tikka 34

Chicken Gilafi Seekh Kabab 37

Shikhampuri Kabab 38

Contd 39

Patther Kabab 40

Jalpari Kabab 41

Contents

Vegetables

Amras ke Malai Aloo 42

Contd 43

Bharwan Bhindi 44

Besan ke Shahi Gatte 45

Diwani Handi 46

Methi Chaman 47

Khatte Baingan 48

Contd 49

Methi Corn Malai 50

Cabbage Chana Dal 51

Khatti Arbi ka Salan 52

Paneer Babycorn Balchao 55

Wadian Aloo 56

Vegetable Kolhapuri 57

Paneer Pasanda 58

Palak Chole 59

Paneer Kofta in Spinach Curry 60

Gobhi Kasoori 61

Lahsooni Tindli 62

Benarasi Bharwan Aloo 65

Chicken, Mutton and Seafood

Hara Masala Murgh 66

Koyla Chicken 67

Murgh Methi Malai 68

Gongura Chicken 69

Murgh Jugalbandi 70

Chicken Jalfraezi 71

Chicken Cafreal 72

Malvani Mutton 75

Mangshor Jhol 76

Gosht Pasanda 77
Laal Maas 78
Dabba Gosht 79
Daab Chingri 80
Malabar Chemeen Kari 81
Prawn Ghassi 82
Pomfret Recheiado 85

Rice and Breads

Narangi Pulao 86
Chicken Kheema Pulao 87
Lucknowi Murgh Biryani 88
Kachche Gosht ki Biryani 89
Contd 90
Chingri Macher Pulao 91
Bakarkhani 92
Onion Paneer Kulcha 93
Sheermal 94
Baida Roti 95
Butter Garlic Naan 96
Rajasthani Baati 97
Missi Roti 98
Kathal Ki Biryani 99
Contd 100
Varqi Parantha 103

Accompaniments

Punj Rattani Dal 104

Lobia Rassedar 105
Sookhi Urad Dal 106
Gujarati Kadhi 107
Ma Chole di Dal 108
Punjabi Kadhi 109
Rajasthani Dal 110
Palak Milakootal 111
Chunda 112
Khajoor di Chutney 113
Tomato Chatni 114
Bhindi Raita 115

Desserts

Balushahi 116
Kaju Katli 117
Chocolate Walnut Burfi 118
Gulab-e-Gulkand 121
Sheer Kurma 122
Chum Chum 123
Choorma Laddoo 124
Besan Burfi 125
Kesar Pista Kulfi with Falooda 126
Glossary 127
Glossary 128
Glossary 129
Glossary 130
Order Form 131
Order Form 132

Ingredients

Pigeon peas split (toovar dal).......3 tbsps		Oil...1 tbsp	
Garlic..................................3 cloves		Salt...to taste	
Curry leaves.........................10		Turmeric powder...........................¼ tsp	
Peppercorns...........................10-12		Tamarind pulp..............................2 tbsps	
Bengal gram split (chana dal).........1 tsp		Jaggery (grated)............................1 tbsp	
Black gram split (dhuli urad dal)....1 tsp		**Tempering**	
Red chillies whole...........................6-7		Oil...1 tbsp	
Fenugreek seeds.............................¼ tsp		Mustard seeds...............................½ tsp	
Cumin seeds...............................½ tsp		Red chillies whole.............................2	
Mustard seeds...............................¾ tsp		Asafoetida.....................................¼ tsp	
Coriander seeds...............................1 tsp		Curry leaves.....................................10	

Method of preparation

1. Wash and soak toovar dal in one cup of water for half an hour and pressure-cook the dal in one cup of water. When cooked mash well and keep aside.
2. Peel, wash and crush garlic. Wash and pat dry curry leaves. Coarsely powder peppercorns.
3. Dry roast and powder the chana dal, urad dal, red chillies, fenugreek seeds, cumin seeds, half a teaspoon of mustard seeds and coriander seeds.
4. Heat oil in a kadai and add garlic, remaining mustard seeds, crushed peppercorns and curry leaves.
5. When the mustard starts to crackle, add mashed dal, the masala powder mixed with a little water, salt, turmeric powder, tamarind pulp and jaggery. Blend well and add five cups of water. Bring to a boil.
6. Simmer on low heat for ten to fifteen minutes. Strain it through a muslin cloth.
7. Heat oil in a pan for tempering. Add mustard seeds, allow them to crackle, add red chillies, asafoetida and curry leaves. Pour over the rasam. Serve hot.

Pepper Rasam

Ingredients

Spinach (palak)	2 bunches	Cinnamon	1 inch stick
Ginger	3 one inch pieces	Refined flour (maida)	2 tbsps
Garlic	5 cloves	Peppercorns	4 – 5
Onion	1 medium sized	Bay leaves	4
Butter	2 tbsps	Salt	to taste
Black cardamoms	3	White pepper powder	¼ tsp
Cloves	2	Roasted cumin powder	1 tsp

Palak Shorba

Method of preparation

1. Clean and wash spinach leaves thoroughly under running water. Blanch the leaves in boiling hot water for two to three minutes. Drain, refresh in cold water and puree them in a mixer.
2. Peel, wash and finely chop ginger, garlic and onion.
3. Heat butter in a deep pan. Add black cardamoms, cloves, cinnamon, refined flour and sauté for two to three minutes.
4. Add chopped ginger, garlic, onion and continue to sauté for about five minutes.
5. Add peppercorns, bay leaves, salt, white pepper powder, roasted cumin powder and five cups of water. Stir and simmer for ten minutes stirring at intervals.
6. Strain the stock. Add the spinach puree to the strained stock and mix well.
7. Cook for four to five minutes. Serve piping hot.

Ingredients

Lemon juice	2 tbsps	Ginger	1 inch piece
Fresh coriander leaves	1 small bunch	Garlic	5 cloves
Gram flour (besan)	2 tbsps	Peppercorns	7-8
Cabbage	¼ small sized	Oil	2 tbsps
Carrot	1 medium sized	Vegetable stock (or water)	2½ cups
Onion	1 medium sized	Salt	to taste
Spring onion bulb	1 medium sized		

Method of preparation

1. Wash cabbage and cut into half centimeter sized cubes. Peel, wash and cut carrot into half centimeter sized cubes.
2. Peel, wash and chop onion, spring onion bulb, ginger and garlic. Clean, wash coriander leaves and reserve the stems. Wash and finely chop coriander leaves. Crush peppercorns.
3. Heat oil in a pan. Add onion, spring onion bulb, ginger and garlic and sauté till translucent. Add gram flour and continue to sauté till you get a nice aroma.
4. Add vegetable stock or water, coriander stems and bring to a boil. Add crushed peppercorns and continue to boil.
5. Add half the chopped coriander leaves and cook for five to ten minutes. Strain and keep aside the cooked vegetables.
6. Heat the strained soup. Add salt, lemon juice and bring to a boil again.
7. Season with the remaining chopped coriander leaves and serve hot.

Note: To make vegetable stock, cook together one medium sized sliced onion, half a medium sized sliced carrot, two inch chopped celery stalk, two cloves of crushed garlic with five cups of water, one bay leaf, five to six peppercorns and two to three cloves for about fifteen minutes. Strain, cool and store in a refrigerator to use when required.

Lemon And Coriander Soup

17

Tomato And Paneer Soup

Ingredients

Tomatoes......................5 medium sized	Oil..2 tsps
Cottage cheese (paneer)...............100 gms	Tomato ketchup............................4 tbsps
Onion........................1 medium sized	Vegetable stock/water.................4 cups
Ginger............................1 inch piece	Salt...to taste
Garlic...............................4 cloves	Peppercorns (crushed)....................¼ tsp
Green chillies.................................1–2	Rice powder...............................½ tbsp
Fresh coriander leaves..........a few sprigs	

Method of preparation

1. Wash and chop tomatoes. Wash and cut paneer into one centimetre sized cubes. Peel, wash and chop onion. Peel, wash and chop ginger and garlic. Remove stems, wash and chop green chillies. Clean, wash and chop coriander leaves.

2. Heat oil, add chopped onion and sauté on high heat. Add ginger and garlic and sauté for some time.

3. Add tomatoes, green chillies and sauté for a minute. Add tomato ketchup and vegetable stock or water and let the mixture boil.

4. Mash the mixture well and strain. Puree the vegetables and add it to the strained stock.

5. Heat the mixture on medium heat and let it simmer. Season with salt and crushed peppercorns.

6. Mix rice flour in half a cup of water and make a smooth paste.

7. Add paneer cubes and rice powder paste to the boiling soup to thicken it. Cook for a minute.

8. Serve piping hot, garnished with chopped coriander leaves.

Note: To make vegetable stock cook together one medium sized sliced onion, half a medium sized sliced carrot, two inch chopped celery stalk, two cloves of crushed garlic with five cups of water, one bay leaf, five to six peppercorns and two to three cloves for about fifteen minutes. Strain, cool and store in a refrigerator to use when required.

Ingredients

Chicken bones	500 gms	Salt	to taste
Chicken (boneless)	100 gms	Rasam powder	2 tbsps
Tomatoes	2 medium sized	Red chilli powder	1 tsp
Fresh coriander leaves	a few sprigs	Turmeric powder	½ tsp
Curry leaves	15	Desi ghee	2 tbsps
Peppercorns	8	Mustard seeds	1 tsp
Coconut (scraped)	½ cup	Red chillies whole	2-3
Tamarind pulp	3 tbsps		

Method of preparation

1. Clean and wash chicken bones. Clean, wash and chop boneless chicken into one inch sized cubes. Wash and roughly chop tomatoes. Clean, wash and chop fresh coriander leaves. Wash and pat dry curry leaves. Crush peppercorns. Grind scraped coconut with one cup of warm water, extract coconut milk and keep aside. Keep the coconut residue too.

2. Boil the chicken bones in about six to seven cups of water for fifteen minutes. Skim the scum from the surface, add tamarind pulp, tomatoes, chicken cubes, salt, rasam powder, crushed peppercorns, red chilli powder, turmeric powder, ten curry leaves and continue cooking.

3. Simmer till the liquid reduces by half and a nice aroma is given out. Add the drained coconut residue to the rasam. Sprinkle coriander leaves and simmer for about three to four minutes. Remove from heat and strain rasam. Cut cooked chicken into one centimetre sized cubes and reserve for garnish.

4. Reheat the strained rasam, add coconut milk and simmer for a couple of minutes. Remove from heat and add chicken pieces to it.

5. Heat ghee and temper it with mustard seeds, red chillies and the remaining curry leaves. Add to the prepared soup and cover immediately to trap the flavours. Serve piping hot. You can squeeze a lemon to make it real tangy.

Note: To make rasam powder heat half a tablespoon of oil in a kadai and sauté three grams of asafoetida and twenty curry leaves for half a minute. Roast separately fifteen whole red chillies, one tablespoon of cumin seeds, two tablespoons of coriander seeds, one teaspoon of fenugreek seeds and one tablespoon of roasted chana dal. Cool, mix and grind to a fine powder. Cool and store in an airtight container for future use.

Chicken Coconut Rasam

Ingredients

Lamb-trotters (paya)......................10-12	Cinnamon......................2 one-inch sticks
Onions..........................4 medium sized	Salt...to taste
Garlic...................................10 cloves	Ghee...½ cup
Fresh coriander leaves.......1 small bunch	Red chilli powder..........................½ tsp
Turmeric powder...........................½ tsp	Pepper powder...............................½ tsp
Cloves...6-8	Garam masala powder...................1 tsp
Green cardamoms...............................4	Lemon juice..................................1 tbsp

Method of preparation

1. Wash payas thoroughly. Peel and wash onions. Cut two onions into quarters and finely slice the remaining. Peel garlic. Make a paste of the quartered onions and garlic. Clean, wash and finely chop coriander leaves.
2. In a large pot add fifteen cups of water and payas. Add onion paste, turmeric powder, cloves, green cardamoms, cinnamon and salt.
3. Cook for four hours on low heat (dum).
4. Boil till the payas are tender. If required, add another two to three cups of water.
5. Heat ghee in a pan and fry sliced onions till golden brown. Add red chilli powder and pepper powder.
6. Add this mixture to the payas and cook for five minutes. Strain the liquid and separate the payas from the residue.
7. Heat the strained liquid with coriander leaves, garam masala powder and the payas.
8. Remove from heat when ghee appears on top. Add lemon juice.
9. Serve with roti/phulka/sheermal.

Paya
Shorba

Ingredients

Green gram (moong) (sprouted).......1 cup	Raw mango........................1 small sized
Mauth (sprouted)...........................1 cup	Cumin seeds (roasted)....................¼ tsp
Salt.......................................to taste	Red chilli powder............................¼ tsp
Turmeric powder...........a generous pinch	Dry mango powder (amchur)..........1 tsp
Onion.............................1 small sized	Oil...1 tbsp
Tomato............................1 small sized	Lemon juice................................2 tsps
Capsicum.........................1 small sized	Chaat masala................................2 tsps
Green chillies...2	

Method of preparation

1. Boil the moong and mauth sprouts separately in two cups of water each with a pinch of salt and a pinch of turmeric powder for about three to four minutes. Drain immediately. Leave them in a colander so that all the water is drained away.

2. Peel, wash and finely chop onion. Wash and chop tomato. Wash, halve, deseed and chop capsicum. Remove stems, wash and finely chop green chillies. Peel, wash and grate raw mango.

3. Mix sprouted moong and mauth with onion, capsicum, tomato, green chillies, roasted cumin seeds, red chilli powder, amchur powder, grated raw mango and oil.

4. Mix lemon juice, chaat masala and salt and pour over salad. Mix well and serve immediately.

Note: Mauth is a brown coloured whole gram which is a little smaller in size than green gram (moong). It is generally sprouted and used. It is known as matki in Maharashtra where matki chi ussal is a very popular dish.

Moong Mauth Chaat

Gajar Aur Kishmish Salad

Ingredients

Carrots	4-5 large sized	Honey	1 tbsp
Raisins	½ cup	Salt	to taste
Green chilli	1	Black salt	¼ tsp
Fresh mint leaves	6–8	Walnut kernels (crushed)	6
Lemon juice	2 tbsps	Oil	1 tsp
Peppercorns (crushed)	¼ tsp		

Method of preparation

1. Peel, wash and thickly grate carrots. Refrigerate till use.
2. Wash, remove stalks of raisins and pat them dry. Remove stem, wash and finely chop green chilli. Clean and wash mint leaves and keep aside for garnishing.
3. Combine lemon juice, crushed peppercorns, green chilli, honey, salt, black salt, walnuts, raisins and oil to make a dressing.
4. Just before serving add the dressing to the grated carrots and toss. Serve garnished with mint leaves.

Ingredients

Chicken (boneless)	250 gms	Onions	2 large sized
Hung yogurt	½ cup	Green capsicum	1 large sized
Ginger	¼ inch piece	Red capsicum	1 large sized
Garlic	2-3 cloves	Yellow capsicum	1 large sized
Green chillies	2-3	Fresh mint leaves	a few sprigs
Salt	to taste	Butter	for basting
Pepper powder	1 tsp	Lemon juice	3 tbsps

Method of preparation

1. Clean, wash and cut chicken into one inch sized cubes. Peel and wash ginger and garlic. Remove stems, wash and roughly chop green chillies. Grind ginger, garlic and green chillies to a fine paste.
2. Marinate chicken pieces in a mixture of hung yogurt, ginger-garlic-green chilli paste, one teaspoon of salt, half a teaspoon of pepper powder for fifteen minutes.
3. Peel, wash and slice onions. Wash, halve, deseed and cut green, red and yellow capsicums into julienne. Clean, wash and tear mint leaves.
4. Preheat the oven to 250°C.
5. Pierce chicken onto skewers and cook in the preheated oven at 250°C for ten to twelve minutes or till done, or alternatively cook in the tandoor till done, basting with butter while cooking. Cool in a refrigerator.
6. In a bowl toss together the chicken, onions, capsicums and salt. Sprinkle lemon juice, garnish with mint leaves and serve cold immediately.

Chef's tip: To make hung yogurt, tie up fresh yogurt in a muslin cloth and hang it with a bowl underneath, preferably in a refrigerator, so that the excess water is drained away completely.

Murgh Shahjahani Chaat

Bhutte Ke Cutlet

Ingredients

Corn niblets......................................1 cup	Turmeric powder............................½ tsp
Onions...........................2 medium sized	Coriander powder............................1 tsp
Green chillies......................................4-6	Red chilli powder............................1 tsp
Ginger..............................2 inch piece	Garam masala powder....................1 tsp
Fresh coriander leaves..½ medium bunch	Salt...to taste
Gram flour (besan).....................¼ cup	Breadcrumbs.................................¼ cup
Oil.....................2 tbsps + to deep-fry	Lemon juice.................................2 tbsps
Cumin seeds......................................1 tsp	Chaat masala..............................2 tbsps
Fennel seeds (saunf)........................1 tsp	

Method of preparation

1. Boil corn niblets or pressure cook them in two cups of water and cool. Squeeze them in a muslin cloth to drain excess water.
2. Peel, wash and chop onions. Remove stems, wash and chop green chillies. Peel, wash and chop ginger. Clean, wash and chop coriander leaves. Roast gram flour in a pan till it gives a nice aroma.
3. Heat two tablespoons of oil in a pan, add cumin seeds and fennel seeds and sauté till they change colour. Add onions and sauté till light brown in colour.
4. Add turmeric powder, coriander powder, red chilli powder and garam masala powder. Stir to mix well. Add half the cooked corn niblets and sauté till dry. Remove from heat, cool slightly and grind in a mixer. Remove into a bowl.
5. Add the rest of the cooked corn niblets, chopped coriander leaves and salt to taste.
6. Add gram flour, breadcrumbs and mix well to form a dough. Make sixteen equal sized cutlets.
7. Heat sufficient oil in a kadai and deep fry the cutlets till golden brown in colour. Drain onto an absorbent kitchen towel.
8. Sprinkle lemon juice and chaat masala and serve hot.

Ingredients

Refined flour (maida)	2 cups	Ghee	3 tbsps
Salt	to taste	Asafoetida	a pinch
Soda bicarbonate	½ tsp	Coriander powder	1 tsp
Oil	5 tbsps	Cumin powder	½ tsp
For filling		Red chilli powder	1 tsp
Black gram split (dhuli urad dal)	½ cup	Fennel (saunf) powder	¼ tsp
Ginger	1 inch piece	Sugar	½ tsp
Green chilli	1	Salt	to taste
Cashewnuts	6-8	Lemon juice	1 tbsp
Raisins	1 tbsp	Oil	to deep fry

Khasta Kachori

Method of preparation

1. Sift the flour, salt and soda bicarbonate together. Add oil and mix well. Knead into a soft dough using sufficient water. Cover with a moist cloth and set aside.

2. Soak the *dhuli urad dal* in two cups of water for an hour. Drain and coarsely grind using a little water.

3. Peel, wash and finely chop ginger. Remove stem, wash and chop green chilli. Roughly chop cashewnuts. Wash raisins and pat them dry.

4. Heat *ghee* in a *kadai* and add the ground *dal*, ginger, green chilli, asafoetida, coriander powder, cumin powder, red chilli powder, fennel powder, cashewnuts and raisins. Cook till all the moisture has dried up.

5. Add sugar, salt and lemon juice. Mix well and remove from heat, let the mixture cool. Divide into sixteen portions.

6. Divide the flour dough into sixteen equal balls. Roll out into small *puris* so that they are thinner around the edges and thicker in the centre.

7. Place a portion of stuffing in the centre and bring the edges together to form a ball. Flatten slightly.

8. Heat sufficient oil in a *kadai* and deep fry *kachoris* on low heat for three to five minutes or until golden brown and crisp.

9. Serve with tamarind *chutney*.

Ingredients

Cottage cheese (paneer)..............500 gms	Gram flour (besan)......................2 tbsps
Oil....................1 tbsp + to shallow fry	Cumin seeds...................................½ tsp
Butter (optional)........................to baste	Peppercorns...6
Green masala	Cloves..6
Fresh coriander leaves.......1 small bunch	Cinnamon powder........................1 tbsp
Green chillies....................................2–3	Rock salt (sendha namak)...........to taste
Ginger....................................1 inch piece	Chaat masala..................................2 tsps
Raw mango.......................1 small sized	

Method of preparation

1. Cut the paneer into one-inch sized cubes.
2. Clean, wash and chop coriander leaves. Remove stems, wash and roughly chop green chillies. Peel, wash and chop ginger. Peel, wash, de-seed and chop raw mango.
3. Dry roast gram flour in pan till it gives out a nice aroma.
4. Grind together coriander leaves, green chillies, ginger, raw mango, cumin seeds, peppercorns, cloves and cinnamon powder to a fine paste adding a little water if required. Add sendha namak and mix well. Add roasted gram flour and one tablespoon of oil. Mix well.
5. Coat the paneer pieces with the above paste and keep aside for fifteen minutes.
6. Heat sufficient oil in a kadai and shallow fry the paneer pieces till they turn light brown on both sides.
7. Drain onto an absorbent paper. Sprinkle with chaat masala and serve hot.
8. Alternatively you can cook the paneer pieces in a preheated oven at 250°C for twenty minutes frequently basting with butter.

Hariyali Paneer

Ingredients

Vermicelli...................................2 cups		Green chillies..2
Potato.......................1 medium sized		Curry leaves..6-8
Carrot........................1 medium sized		Oil...4 tbsps
French beans...............................5-6		Mustard seeds...........................½ tsp
Cauliflower............................5-6 florets		Black gram split (dhuli urad dal)...2 tsps
Capsicum......................1 medium sized		Turmeric powder.........................¼ tsp
Green peas...............................¼ cup		Salt...to taste
Ginger.................................1 inch piece		Lemon juice...............................2 tbsps
Onion...........................1 medium sized		

Method of preparation

1. Peel, wash and cut potato and carrot into one-centimeter cubes. String, wash and cut French beans into one-centimeter pieces. Wash cauliflower florets. Wash, halve, deseed and cut capsicum into one-centimeter cubes. Wash green peas.
2. Peel, wash and finely chop ginger and onion. Remove stems, wash and slit green chillies. Wash curry leaves and pat them dry.
3. Boil potato, carrot and cauliflower in two cups of water till nearly done. Add French beans and peas and boil further for five minutes. Drain and cool.
4. Heat five cups of water, bring it to a boil, add vermicelli, salt and two tablespoons of oil. Cook for one minute or till slightly underdone. Drain, refresh under cold water and keep aside.
5. Heat remaining oil in a pan, temper with mustard seeds and curry leaves. Add dhuli urad dal, ginger and onion. Sauté well till the onion turns light brown.
6. Add green chillies and stir. Add the cooked vegetables, capsicum, turmeric powder and sauté for four to five minutes.
7. Add cooked vermicelli, salt and stir gently. Cook for five to six minutes.
8. Remove from heat. Mix in lemon juice and serve hot.

Vegetable Vermicelli Upma

Crunchy Paneer Pakora

Ingredients

Cottage cheese (paneer)...............250 gms
Oil...................................to deep fry
Boondi..................................1 cup

For garlic chutney
Garlic.............................8–10 cloves
Oil..1 tsp
Red chilli powder.........................1 tbsp
Salt...................................to taste

For the batter
Gram flour (besan).........................1 cup
Garlic..............................1½ inch piece
Ginger ....5 cloves
Red chilli powder...........................1 tsp
Turmeric powder...........................½ tsp
Soda bicarbonate........................a pinch
Salt...................................to taste

Method of preparation

1. Wash and cut cottage cheese into two inch by half inch by half inch sized batons. Slit each baton into half leaving one edge intact for filling.
2. Crush the boondi with your hand and keep aside.
3. To make garlic chutney, peel and roast garlic in one teaspoon of oil. Mix with red chilli powder and salt and grind to a smooth paste.
4. To prepare batter, peel and wash ginger and garlic and grind together to make a paste. Mix gram flour with this paste, red chilli powder, turmeric powder, soda bicarbonate and salt. Add sufficient water and whisk well to make a batter of coating consistency. Rest the batter for about fifteen minutes.
5. Stuff garlic chutney into the slit of each cottage cheese baton.
6. Heat sufficient oil in a kadai, dip each baton of cottage cheese into the batter, roll in the crushed boondi and deep fry on medium heat till crisp and golden brown. Drain onto an absorbent paper.
7. Serve hot with a chutney of your choice.

Ingredients

Whole wheat grain (gehun)............1 cup	Oil............................2 tsps + to deep fry
Rice...1 cup	Green chillies...................................2-3
Black gram split (dhuli urad dal)..¼ cup	Ginger ....1 inch piece
Green gram split (moong dal)........¼ cup	Fresh coriander leaves.......1 small bunch
Bengal gram split (chana dal).......¼ cup	Turmeric powder ....½ tsp
Salt...to taste	Sugar..½ tsp
Sodabicarbonate.........................a pinch	Asafoetida..................................a pinch
Yogurt...¼ cup	

Method of preparation

1. Grind wheat, rice and the dals coarsely without adding any water.
2. Add salt, sodabicarbonate, yogurt, two teaspoons of oil and little warm water to the coarsely ground flour mixture and make a thick batter using water.
3. Cover with a cloth and keep it in a warm place to ferment for eight to ten hours.
4. Remove stems and wash green chillies. Peel and wash ginger. Grind them together into a fine paste. Clean, wash and finely chop coriander leaves.
5. Add ginger-green chilli paste, turmeric powder, sugar, coriander leaves and asafoetida to the fermented batter. Mix well.
6. Heat sufficient oil in a kadai. Drop tablespoonsful of batter into the hot oil and deep fry till golden and crisp.
7. Drain onto an absorbent paper and serve hot with any chutney of your choice.

Kathiawadi Vada

31

Ingredients

Cottage cheese (paneer)	500 gms	Lemon juice	1 tbsp
Ginger	¾ inch piece	Green cardamom powder	½ tsp
Garlic	5 cloves	Lucknowi fennel (saunf) powder	½ tsp
Oil	2 tsps	Saffron (kesar)	a few strands
Gram flour (besan)	2 tbsps	Fresh cream	1 cup
Turmeric powder	½ tsp	Butter	for basting
White pepper powder	1 tsp	Chaat masala	1 ½ tsps
Salt	to taste	Lemon juice	1 tbsp

Method of preparation

1. Wash and cut paneer into one and a half inch sized squares of half inch thickness. Peel, wash and grind ginger and garlic.
2. Heat oil in a pan. Add besan and cook until it emits a fragrant aroma, remove from heat and add turmeric powder. Cool the flour and transfer into a bowl.
3. Add ginger and garlic paste, white pepper powder, salt, lemon juice, green cardamom powder, fennel powder, saffron and cream. Whisk well to make a batter.
4. Add paneer cubes to the batter and marinate for at least an hour.
5. Thread paneer cubes onto skewers two centimeters apart.
6. Roast in a tandoor/charcoal grill for five minutes, basting with melted butter occasionally till the tikkas are golden in colour.
7. Alternatively you can cook the tikkas in a convection oven or on a grill. Preheat the oven to 220°C and cook for three minutes on either side, basting once with butter in between.
8. Remove and sprinkle with chaat masala powder and lemon juice. Serve with chutney of your choice.

Saunfia
Paneer
Tikka

Ingredients

Papads..8	Red chilli powder...........................½ tsp
Potatoes........................4 medium sized	Cumin powder...............................1 tsp
Peas (shelled)...............................¼ cup	Turmeric powder...........................½ tsp
Ginger................................1 inch piece	Chaat masala.................................1 tsp
Fresh coriander leaves.......1 small bunch	Salt...to taste
Oil.......................1½ tbsps + to deep fry	Gram flour (besan)....................2 tbsps
Cumin seeds.....................................1 tsp	

Papad Rolls

Method of preparation

1. Wash and boil potatoes in sufficient water. Cool, peel and mash.
2. Wash and drain green peas. Parboil the peas in half a cup of salted water. Drain.
3. Wash, peel and finely chop ginger. Clean, wash and finely chop coriander leaves.
4. Heat one and a half tablespoons of oil in a pan and add cumin seeds. When they change colour add ginger, parboiled green peas and stir fry for a minute.
5. Add red chilli powder, cumin powder, turmeric powder, chaat masala and sauté for half a minute.
6. Add this to the mashed potatoes along with salt and chopped coriander leaves and mix. Divide into eight equal portions. Make a paste of gram flour with one tablespoon of water.
7. Place one portion of the potato mixture on one side of a papad and spread evenly. Apply gram flour paste on the edges of the papad and roll. Fold the edges of the papad inwards taking care that the potato mixture does not come out.
8. Heat sufficient oil in a kadai and deep fry papad rolls for about a minute till crisp. Drain onto an absorbent paper and serve hot.

Ingredients

Chicken (boneless)...........................½ kg	Hung yogurt...................................1 cup
Peppercorns...............................12–15	Fresh cream.................................3 tbsps
Onions.........................4 medium sized	Cornstarch..................................1 tbsp
Ginger ....1 inch piece	Egg white..1
Garlic...................................6–8 cloves	Garam masala powder..................½ tsp
Green chilli...................................2–3	Salt..to taste
Oil...4 tbsps	Green cardamom powder...............¼ tsp
Green capsicum.............1 medium sized	Butter ....for basting

Method of preparation

1. Trim, wash and cut chicken into one and a half-inch sized cubes. Pat them dry. Dry roast peppercorns and crush to a coarse powder.
2. Peel, wash and slice onions. Peel and wash ginger and garlic. Remove stems, wash and roughly chop green chillies. Grind ginger, garlic and green chillies to a fine paste.
3. Heat oil in a kadai and sauté onions till brown. Cool and grind to a paste. Wash, halve, de-seed and cut capsicum into one inch sized pieces.
4. In a large bowl combine browned onion paste, hung yogurt, fresh cream, cornstarch, egg white, ginger, garlic, green chilli paste, garam masala powder, capsicum cubes, crushed peppercorns, salt, green cardamom powder. Add chicken cubes, mix well and allow to marinate for one hour preferably in the refrigerator.
5. Preheat oven to 180°C.
6. Arrange the chicken cubes and capsicum cubes alternately on a skewer and cook in the preheated oven at 250°C for fifteen minutes basting occasionally with butter.
7. Serve hot with onion rings and mint chutney.

Chef's tip: To make hung yogurt, tie up fresh yogurt in a muslin cloth and hang it with a bowl underneath, preferably in a refrigerator, so that the excess water is drained away completely.

Kalimirch Tikka

Ingredients

Chicken mince.....................½ kg	Garam masala powder....................1 tsp
Onions.....................2 large sized	Lemon juice.....................1 tsp
Oil.....................to deep fry	Salt.....................to taste
Ginger.....................1½ inch piece	Cashewnut powder.....................1 tbsp
Garlic.....................10 cloves	Cashewnuts (whole).....................10-12
Fresh coriander leaves..........a few sprigs	Egg.....................1
Fresh mint leaves.....................15-20	Butter.....................for basting
Green chillies.....................2-3	Lemon wedges.....................for garnish
Red chilli powder.....................1 tsp	

Method of preparation

1. Wash chicken mince and press between the palms of your hand to remove excess water.
2. Peel, wash and finely slice onions. Heat sufficient oil in a kadai and deep-fry the onions until golden brown in colour. Drain onto an absorbent paper and keep aside.
3. Peel, wash and grind ginger and garlic to a fine paste. Clean, wash and finely chop coriander leaves. Clean, wash, reserve a few mint leaves for garnishing and finely chop the rest. Remove stems, wash and finely chop green chillies.
4. In a large bowl combine chicken mince, browned onions, chopped coriander leaves, chopped mint leaves, ginger and garlic paste, chopped green chillies, red chilli powder, garam masala powder, lemon juice and salt.
5. Mix and blend all the above ingredients in a mixer for half a minute.
6. Remove the mixture into a bowl and add cashewnut powder. Mix well, cover and allow it to stand for half an hour preferably in a refrigerator.
7. Coarsely grind the whole cashewnuts in a mixer. Beat egg, mix it along with the coarsely ground cashewnuts and keep it aside.
8. Divide mince mixture into twenty equal portions. Preheat oven to 250°C or light a tandoor.
9. Using wet hands dab the mince mixture onto skewers in a cylindrical shape, one inch apart, making each kabab three inches long.
10. Cook in a preheated oven at 250°C for twelve to fifteen or in tandoor for eight to ten minutes till half done. Brush it with the egg and cashewnut mixture and cook till done, basting it with butter occasionally.
11. Serve hot, garnished with lemon wedges and reserved mint leaves.

Note: It is important to have some juice in the kabab, otherwise it would taste very dry. Do not overcook.

Chicken Gilafi Seekh Kabab

Ingredients

Mutton mince...............................2 cups	Garam masala powder....................1 tsp
Bengal gram (chana dal)...............½ cup	Lemon juice..............................1 tbsp
Kashmiri red chillies.........................3-4	Sesame seeds..............................1 tbsp
Cinnamon...........................1 inch stick	Oil...............................to shallow fry
Cloves..3-4	Eggs..2
Peppercorns.....................................5-6	**For stuffing**
Cumin seeds..................................1 tbsp	Yogurt...1 cup
Coriander seeds.............................1 tbsp	Onion........................1 large sized
Green chillies.......................................2	Green chilli..1
Ginger ....1 inch piece	Fresh mint leaves................a few sprigs
Garlic....................................4-5 cloves	Salt...............................to taste
Salt..to taste	Cumin seeds (roasted)....................½ tsp

Method of preparation

1. Wash mutton mince and squeeze between the palm of your hands to remove excess water. Wash and soak chana dal in one cup of water for an hour. Drain and keep aside.
2. Dry roast Kashmiri red chillies, cinnamon, cloves, peppercorns, cumin seeds, coriander seeds and grind to a fine powder.
3. Remove stems, wash and finely chop green chillies. Peel, wash and finely chop ginger and garlic.
4. In a large pan combine mutton mince, chana dal, chopped green chillies, chopped ginger and garlic and salt to taste. Add two cups of water and bring to a boil. Reduce heat, add the powdered masala and allow to simmer on low heat till almost done and the mixture is dry. Remove from heat and allow to cool. When cool grind the mixture to a paste.
5. Add garam masala powder and lemon juice to the ground paste and mix well. Add sesame seeds to the mutton mixture and mix well. Divide into sixteen portions.

Shikhampuri Kabab

6. For stuffing, hang yogurt in a muslin cloth for an hour preferably in a refrigerator till most of the moisture has drained away. Peel, wash and chop onion. Remove stem, wash and chop green chilli. Clean, wash and chop mint leaves. Add green chilli, onion, mint leaves, salt and roasted cumin seeds to the yogurt. Mix well and divide into sixteen equal portions.
7. Flatten one portion of the mince mixture in the palm of your hand and place a portion of yogurt stuffing in the centre. Gather the edges, shape into a roundel and flatten slightly. Similarly shape the rest of the kababs.
8. Beat eggs and keep in a bowl. Heat a little oil in a pan. Dip each kabab into the beaten egg and shallow fry the kababs till golden brown.
9. Drain onto an absorbent paper and serve hot with onion rings and mint chutney.

(See Photo on Page 36)

Ingredients

Mutton (boneless)......................800 gms	Pepper powder..............................1 tsp
For marinade	Green cardamom powder.................1 tsp
Ginger..............................2 inch piece	Garam masala powder....................1 tsp
Garlic......................................10 cloves	Lichen stone flower (patthar ke phool)
Green chillies...................................5	powder..1 tsp
Raw papaya........................3 inch piece	Malt vinegar...............................1 tbsp
Onions...........................2 medium sized	Salt...to taste
Oil.................4 tbsps + to deep fry	Oil or ghee.............................for basting
Yogurt...2 tbsps	

Method of preparation

Patther Kabab

1. Clean, wash and pat dry mutton. Cut into one inch by one and a half inch pieces. Pound gently with a steak hammer or the blunt side of a knife to half a centimetre thickness.
2. Peel and wash ginger and garlic. Remove stems and wash green chillies. Peel, wash and chop raw papaya. Grind ginger, garlic, green chillies and raw papaya to a fine paste.
3. Peel, wash and slice onions. Heat sufficient oil in a kadai and deep-fry sliced onions till brown. Drain, cool and grind to a fine paste with yogurt.
4. Mix together ginger-garlic-green chillies-papaya paste, browned onion paste, pepper powder, green cardamom powder, garam masala powder, lichen stone flower powder, malt vinegar and four tablespoons of oil. Mix well and apply uniformly on the mutton pasandas. Let it marinate for three to four hours, preferably in a refrigerator.

Cooking on stone slabs: (traditional way of cooking on kadappa stone.)

5. Take a flat piece of rough granite or kadappa of about one and a half feet length χ one-foot breadth χ two-inch thickness.
6. Wash the stone and rest it on bricks kept on two sides to make a bridge, taking care that it is safely balanced.
7. Heat the granite well with live charcoals underneath. Season the stone by applying oil when it is very hot. Then sprinkle a little salt and wipe with a clean cloth. It's now ready to use.
8. Sprinkle a little oil or ghee on the surface and place the marinated mutton.
9. Turn them a few times basting them occasionally with oil. Remove when cooked through.
10. Serve with hot tandoori rotis and kachumber salad.

Chef's tip: It can be grilled on a non-stick tawa.

Ingredients

Fish fillets............................8
Shrimps..............................½ cup
Prawns......................8 medium sized
Butter..........................for basting

First marinade (fish)

Ginger............................½ inch piece
Garlic..................................5 cloves
Hung yogurt........................1 cup
Fresh cream........................½ cup
Carom seeds (ajwain)...................1 tsp
Egg..1
Garam masala powder.................1 tsp
Lemon juice........................1 tbsp
Oil....................................1 tbsp
Salt....................................to taste

Second marinade (for shrimps and prawns)

Ginger ....½ inch piece
Garlic..................................5 cloves
Hung yogurt........................¾ cup
Red chilli powder............................1 tsp
Turmeric powder....................¼ tsp
Carom seed (ajwain)......................1 tsp
Egg...1
Fresh cream........................½ cup
Garam masala powder..................¼ tsp
Lemon juice...............................1 tsp
Oil...................................1 tbsp
Salt................................to taste
Cheese (grated)............................½ cup

Method of preparation

1. Trim, wash, pat dry and flatten fish fillets using a steak hammer. Shell, de-vein and wash shrimps thoroughly. Shell prawns leaving the tails intact, de-vein and wash thoroughly. Squeeze the shrimps and prawns between the palm of your hands to remove excess moisture.

2. For the first marinade, peel, wash and grind ginger and garlic into a fine paste. Mix with rest of the ingredients. Apply this marinade on both sides of the fish fillets and allow to stand for half an hour, preferably in a refrigerator.

3. For the second marinade, peel, wash and grind ginger and garlic into a fine paste. Mix all the ingredients of the second marinade, divide into two portions and marinade prawns and shrimps separately for half an hour, preferably in a refrigerator.

4. Preheat oven to 240°C.

5. To prepare the kababs place two marinated shrimps and a prawn at the centre of the marinated fish fillet leaving the tail of the prawn on the outer edge. Roll and secure with a toothpick.

6. Arrange on skewers and cook in a tandoor for eight to ten minutes, basting occasionally with butter.

7. Alternatively, cook in the preheated oven at 240°C for ten to twelve minutes basting occasionally with butter.

8. Serve hot with mint chutney.

Jalpari
Kabab

Amras Ke Malai Aloo

Ingredients

Baby potatoes	20-25	Cloves	3-4
Oil	3 tbsps + to deep fry	Turmeric powder	¼ tsp
Green chillies	2	Red chilli powder	½ tsp
Onions	2 large sized	Ripe mango pulp	1/3 cup
Ginger	¼ inch piece	Salt	to taste
Garlic	2 cloves	Garam masala powder	1 tsp
Watermelon seeds	1 tsp	Lemon juice	1 tsp
Muskmelon seeds	1 tsp	**Grind**	
Yogurt	¾ cup	Caraway seeds (shahi jeera)	¼ tsp
Saffron	few strands	Peppercorns	6-8
Fresh cream	2 tbsps	Green cardamoms	2
Caraway seeds (shahi jeera)	1 tsp	Cloves	2-3
Green cardamoms	3-4		

Method of preparation

1. Wash and scrub potatoes under running water. Prick them with a fork. Pat dry.
2. Heat sufficient oil in a kadai and deep fry them along with the skin till golden. Drain onto a kitchen towel and keep aside.
3. Remove stems, wash and slit green chillies. Peel, wash and grind onions into a smooth paste. Peel, wash and grind ginger and garlic to a smooth paste. Lightly roast watermelon seeds and muskmelon seeds and grind to a paste using a little water. Whisk yogurt and keep aside. Dissolve saffron in fresh cream and keep aside.
4. Heat three tablespoons of oil in a pan, add shahi jeera, green cardamoms and cloves. When they change colour add green chillies and onion paste and sauté for three to four minutes or till it turns golden brown.
5. Add ginger and garlic paste and sauté for two minutes. Add whisked yogurt, ground melon seeds paste, turmeric powder, red chilli powder and stir-fry till the oil leaves the masala. Add half a cup of water and mix well.

6. When the water comes to a boil add mango pulp, fried potatoes and salt. Stir well.
7. In another pan dry roast shahi jeera, peppercorns, green cardamoms and cloves and grind to a powder.
8. Add garam masala powder, saffron dissolved in fresh cream to the gravy and simmer for a couple of minutes. Adjust seasoning.
9. Add freshly ground masala and lemon juice and stir. Serve hot with paranthas.

Ingredients

Ladyfingers (bhindi)....................500 gms	Dry mango powder (amchur).......2 tbsps
Onions...........................4 medium sized	Turmeric powder.............................1 tsp
Red chilli powder............................1 tbsp	Salt...to taste
Coriander powder........................2 tbsps	Oil...2 tbsps
Cumin powder..............................1 tbsp	

Method of preparation

1. Wash and wipe ladyfingers absolutely dry. Remove head and tail, slit and keep aside. Peel, wash and slice onions thinly.
2. Mix red chilli powder, coriander powder, cumin powder, dry mango powder, turmeric powder and salt in a bowl.
3. Stuff the ladyfingers with this masala. Keep the leftover masala separately.
4. Heat oil in a kadai. Add sliced onions and cook for half a minute. Add stuffed ladyfingers and mix. Cook covered on low heat for five minutes stirring occasionally.
5. Add rest of the dry masala when ladyfingers are almost cooked.
6. Cover and cook till done. Serve hot.

Note: Ensure that you do not add any water to this vegetable.

Bharwan Bhindi

Ingredients

Gram flour (besan)	2½ cups	Salt	to taste
Cottage cheese (paneer) (grated)	½ cup	Sodabicarbonate	¼ tsp
Khoya/mawa (grated)	½ cup	Oil	2 tbsps
Yogurt	2 cups	Cumin seeds	1 tsp
Red chilli powder	1½ tsps	Fenugreek seeds	¼ tsp
Turmeric powder	½ tsp	Peppercorns	8–10
Ginger	1 inch piece	Red chillies whole	3
Green chillies	4	Asafoetida	a pinch
Fresh coriander leaves	a few sprigs	Garam masala powder	½ tsp

Besan Ke Shahi Gatte

Method of preparation

1. Whisk yogurt with two cups of water, two tablespoons of besan, red chilli powder and turmeric powder.

2. Peel, wash and finely chop ginger. Remove stems, wash and finely chop green chillies. Clean, wash and finely chop coriander leaves and reserve for garnish.

3. Mix remaining besan with chopped ginger, salt and sodabicarbonate. Add enough water and knead into a hard dough. Knead well and keep aside for five minutes.

4. In a bowl, mix grated paneer, khoya, half the chopped green chillies and salt. Mix well and keep aside.

5. Divide the besan dough into sixteen equal sized portions. Flatten each portion and stuff paneer-khoya mixture into them. Give a cylindrical shape. Repeat the same procedure for the remaining dough.

6. In a pan, boil water and add the stuffed gattes. Boil for ten to fifteen minutes. Drain and cut into one inch pieces.

7. Heat oil in a kadai, add cumin seeds and stir fry till they change colour. Add fenugreek seeds, peppercorns, whole red chillies broken into two, remaining chopped green chillies, asafoetida and sauté for a minute.

8. Add the whisked yogurt, stirring continuously for three to four minutes until it thickens a little. Add garam masala powder and adjust seasoning. Add water if required.

9. Add cooked gattes to the gravy and continue cooking till the gravy thickens.

10. Garnish with chopped coriander leaves and serve hot.

Note: After boiling the gattes, you can deep fry them and then add it to the gravy.

Ingredients

Potatoes	3 medium sized	Fresh fenugreek leaves (methi)	½ bunch
Carrots	3 medium sized	Fresh coriander leaves	a few sprigs
French beans	10-12	Green chillies	2–3
Broad beans (sem ki phalli)	10-12	Oil	3 tbsps
Brinjals	4-6 small sized	Red chilli powder	1 tsp
Onions	2 medium sized	Turmeric powder	½ tsp
Ginger	1½ inch piece	Salt	to taste
Garlic	10 cloves	Yogurt	2 tbsps
Green peas (shelled)	½ cup	Garam masala powder	½ tsp

Diwani Handi

Method of preparation

1. Peel, wash and cut potatoes and carrots into half inch sized cubes. String, wash and cut French beans and broad beans diagonally. Wash and slit brinjals into two. Peel, wash and thinly slice onions. Peel, wash and grind ginger and garlic to a fine paste. Wash and drain green peas.
2. Clean, wash and chop fresh fenugreek leaves and coriander leaves. Remove stems, wash, de-seed and chop green chillies.
3. Heat oil in a handi, add onions and sauté till light brown. Add green chillies, ginger and garlic paste and sauté for a minute. Add red chilli powder, turmeric powder, salt and mix.
4. Add yogurt and stir-fry for two to three minutes.
5. Add all the vegetables and simmer, covered, till the vegetables are cooked.
6. Add fenugreek leaves, coriander leaves and garam masala powder, stir and cook for three to four minutes.
7. Serve hot with Hyderabadi parantha or any other Indian bread of your choice.

Ingredients

Spinach (palak)............1 medium bunch	Red chilli powder...........................1 tsp
Fresh fenugreek leaves (methi)...............	Ghee...4 tbsps
.....................................1 medium bunch	Caraway seeds (shahi jeera)...........½ tsp
Cottage cheese (paneer).............150 gms	Dry ginger powder (soonth)..........¼ tsp
Garlic.................................3–4 cloves	Green cardamom powder...............¼ tsp
Buttermilk....................................1 cup	White pepper powder....................¼ tsp
Turmeric powder...........................¼ tsp	Salt..to taste

Method of preparation

1. Clean, remove stalk and wash spinach and fenugreek leaves thoroughly. Chop them separately. Blanch the fenugreek leaves. Drain and squeeze to remove excess water.
2. Cut paneer into half inch sized cubes. Peel, wash and finely chop garlic. Mix in turmeric powder and red chilli powder with buttermilk.
3. Heat ghee in a kadai, fry paneer cubes to a golden brown and drain onto an absorbent paper.
4. In the same ghee, add caraway seeds and stir fry for ten seconds. Add chopped garlic and sauté till light brown. Add chopped spinach and sauté for five minutes.
5. Add blanched fenugreek leaves and stir fry for three to four minutes. Add the buttermilk and mix. Cook for a further two to three minutes.
6. Add paneer cubes and mix. Sprinkle dry ginger powder, cardamom powder, white pepper powder, salt and stir fry for two minutes. Serve hot with rice.

Methi Chaman

Khatte Baingan

Ingredients

Small brinjals......................................16
Fresh coriander leaves..........a few sprigs

For the stuffing

Onions......................2 medium sized
Green chillies...6
Ginger......................1 inch piece
Garlic......................5 cloves
Tamarind..........a large lemon sized ball
Oil......................2 tbsps + 1 tsp
Salt......................to taste
Coriander powder......................1 tsp
Cumin powder......................½ tsp

Turmeric powder......................¼ tsp
Garam masala powder....................½ tsp

For tempering

Garlic......................8 cloves
Curry leaves......................8
Yogurt......................½ cup
Oil......................1 tbsp
Red chillies whole......................6
Carom seeds (ajwain)....................¼ tsp
Mustard seeds......................¼ tsp
Cumin seeds......................¼ tsp

Method of preparation

1. Wash and slit brinjals into four, without cutting them through and keeping the stalk intact. Soak in water. Clean, wash and chop coriander leaves.

2. For the stuffing, peel, wash and slice onions finely. Remove stems, wash and finely cut green chillies. Peel, wash and grind ginger and garlic to a smooth paste.

3. Soak tamarind in warm water for about half an hour, squeeze and strain the pulp.

4. In a frying pan, heat two tablespoons of oil, add onions and stir-fry until translucent. Add ginger-garlic paste, stir-fry until devoid of raw flavours. Add green chillies and stir.

5. Add tamarind pulp, salt, coriander powder, cumin powder and turmeric powder. Stir-fry till oil separates.

6. Sprinkle garam masala and remove. Set aside to cool. Preheat the oven to 225 ° C.

7. Grind the masala in a blender to a fine paste. Stuff the masala in between the slits of the brinjals and keep aside.

8. Brush a baking tray with one teaspoon of oil, arrange the brinjals and bake them for fifteen minutes at 225°C. Alternatively shallow fry, covered, in a frying pan.
9. Once cooked remove them onto a serving platter.
10. For the tempering, peel and wash garlic cloves. Wash and pat dry curry leaves. Whisk the yogurt and keep aside.
11. In a frying pan heat one tablespoon of oil, add whole red chillies, garlic cloves, carom seeds, mustard seeds, cumin seeds and curry leaves in that order. Once the garlic gets a little brown, remove from heat, add the yogurt and immediately pour over the brinjals.
12. Garnish with chopped coriander leaves and serve with roomali rotis.

Ingredients

Fresh fenugreek leaves (methi)................1 medium bunch	Oil..2 tbsps
Sweet corn kernels.........................1 cup	Caraway seeds (shahi jeera)...........½ tsp
Salt..to taste	Dry mango powder (amchur).........½ tsp
Onions.........................2 medium sized	White pepper powder....................¼ tsp
Green chillies....................................3	Fresh cream (malai).......................1 cup
Ginger................................½ inch piece	Kasuri methi (crushed)....................1 tsp
Garlic...5 cloves	Green cardamom powder...............¼ tsp

Method of preparation

1. Clean and wash methi leaves thoroughly. You may apply some salt and keep it for some time before washing. Chop methi leaves roughly. Peel, wash and chop onions. Remove stems, wash and chop green chillies. Peel, wash and grind ginger and garlic to a fine paste.
2. Heat oil in a pan, add caraway seeds and stir-fry for ten seconds. Add chopped onions and cook till they are translucent.
3. Add chopped green chillies and stir-fry for ten seconds. Add ginger and garlic paste and methi leaves. Cook, uncovered, for about six to seven minutes.
4. Add sweet corn and cook for three to four minutes. Add amchur, white pepper powder, salt and stir.
5. Add fresh cream and simmer till reduced to half. Sprinkle crushed kasuri methi and green cardamom powder. Mix and serve immediately.

Note: If after adding cream the gravy turns dry, add half a cup of water.

Methi
Corn
Malai

Cabbage Chana Dal

Ingredients

Cabbage.........................1 medium sized	Red chillies whole..................................4
Bengal gram split (chana dal)........¼ cup	Turmeric powder............................½ tsp
Ginger...............................1 inch piece	Salt.....................................to taste
Curry leaves..............................10–12	Garam masala powder...................1 tsp
Oil...2 tbsps	Coconut (scraped)........................2 tbsps
Mustard seeds................................1 tsp	

Method of preparation

1. Clean, wash and soak chana dal in one cup of water for half an hour. Drain and boil chana dal in approximately one cup of water till just done. Drain and keep aside.

2. Wash and shred cabbage. Peel, wash and chop ginger finely. Wash curry leaves and pat them dry.

3. Heat oil. Add mustard seeds, curry leaves and whole red chillies. When the seeds crackle add chopped ginger. Sauté for a minute.

4. Add cabbage and cook until soft. Add turmeric powder and salt and mix. Add boiled chana dal and mix well. Let it cook for two minutes. Add garam masala powder and mix.

5. Garnish with scraped coconut and serve hot.

Ingredients

Colocassia (arbi)	20 – 25 (250 gms)	Oil	3 tbsps
Onion	1 medium sized	Paanch phoron	1 tsp
Ginger	¾ inch piece	Tamarind pulp	2 tbsps
Garlic	7-8 cloves	Turmeric powder	½ tsp
Green chillies	2-3	Red chilli powder	1 tsp
Curry leaves	8-10	Coriander powder	1 tsp
Fresh coriander leaves	a few sprigs	Cumin powder	1 tsp
Peanuts	3 tbsps	Salt	to taste
Sesame seeds (til)	1 tbsp		

Khatti Arbi Ka Salan

Method of preparation

1. Boil arbi in four cups of salted water till tender. Peel, slice the bigger ones into two pieces if desired.
2. Peel, wash and slice onions. Peel, wash and grind ginger and garlic to a fine paste. Remove stems, wash, de-seed and chop green chillies. Wash curry leaves and pat dry. Clean, wash and chop coriander leaves.
3. Roast peanuts and sesame seeds separately until lightly browned. Cool and grind to a fine paste with a little water.
4. Heat oil in a pan, add paanch phoron. Stir fry till the seeds splutter. Add curry leaves and sliced onions and sauté till onions turn golden brown. Add green chillies, ginger and garlic paste and sauté for a few minutes.
5. Add tamarind pulp, turmeric powder, red chilli powder, coriander powder, cumin powder and sauté for three to four minutes on low heat.
6. Add the peanut-sesame seed paste and stir-fry till oil separates. Add two cups of water and simmer for about three to four minutes.
7. Add arbi and salt to taste. Simmer further for five minutes
8. Sprinkle chopped coriander leaves and serve hot with Hyderabadi parantha.

Note: Paanch phoron is a mixture of equal quantities of mustard seeds, cumin seeds, fenugreek seeds, fennel seeds and onion seeds.

Ingredients

Cottage cheese (paneer)	½ kg	Cloves	7–8
Baby corns	7–8	Mustard seeds	1 tsp
Onions	2 medium sized	Cinnamon	1 inch stick
Tomatoes	2 medium sized	Salt	to taste
Ginger	1 inch piece	Malt vinegar	½ cup
Garlic	8–10 cloves	Oil	2 tbsps
Red chillies whole	10–12	Tomato puree	¾ cup
Cumin seeds	1 tsp	Sugar	1 tbsp

Method of preparation

1. Wash and cut *paneer* into diamond shaped pieces. Wash baby corns and boil them in sufficient water for two to three minutes. Drain and cut into small pieces.

2. Peel, wash and chop onions. Wash and chop tomatoes. Peel, wash and roughly chop ginger and garlic.

3. Grind whole red chillies, garlic, ginger, cumin seeds, cloves, mustard seeds, cinnamon and salt with a quarter cup of malt vinegar to a fine paste.

4. Heat oil in a pan, add onions and sauté till light brown. Add tomatoes and mix. Cook for five minutes stirring well.

5. Add baby corns, tomato puree and ground *masala*. Cook for three to four minutes. Add sugar, adjust salt and mix well.

6. Add *paneer* pieces and remaining malt vinegar and cook for five to seven minutes.

7. Serve hot.

Ingredients

Urad dal dried nuggets (wadian)..2-3 big sized	Cumin seeds..................................1 tsp
Potatoes......................4 medium sized	Asafoetida..................................a pinch
Onion.............................1 large sized	Turmeric powder..........................½ tsp
Ginger.....................2 one inch piece	Coriander powder.........................2 tsps
Green chillies...2	Cumin powder..............................½ tsp
Tomatoes.....................2 large sized	Red chilli powder......................1½ tsps
Fresh coriander leaves.........a few sprigs	Salt...to taste
Oil...5 tbsps	Garam masala powder..................½ tsp

Wadian Aloo

Method of preparation

1. Break wadian into small pieces.
2. Wash and cut potatoes without peeling into eight pieces each.
3. Peel, wash and chop onion and one piece of ginger. Peel, wash and cut the other piece of ginger into julienne. Remove stems, wash and slit green chillies. Wash and finely chop tomatoes. Clean, wash and chop coriander leaves.
4. Heat three tablespoons of oil in a pan, add broken wadian and roast till it emits a fragrant aroma. Remove onto an absorbent paper and then soak in a cup of water.
5. Heat two tablespoons of oil in another pan, add cumin seeds and onion and sauté for three minutes.
6. Add ginger, asafoetida, potatoes, turmeric powder, coriander powder, cumin powder, red chilli powder and salt.
7. Stir and add three cups of water. Add wadian. Cover and cook till potatoes are done.
8. Add tomatoes and slit green chillies and cook for five minutes.
9. Sprinkle garam masala powder, ginger julienne and chopped coriander leaves and serve hot.

(See Photo on Page 54)

Ingredients

Carrot..............................1 medium sized	Coriander seeds...............................1 tsp
Potato............................1 medium sized	Red chillies whole (Sankeshwari)........6
Cauliflower.........................6-8 florets	Red chilli powder (Sankeshwari) ....
French beans................................6-8	....1½ tsps
Green peas............................¼ cup	Turmeric powder............................1 tsp
Onions.........................2 large sized	Salt.....................................to taste
Ginger............................½ inch piece	**For Kolhapuri garam masala**
Garlic.............................5-6 cloves	Aniseed (saunf)..........................½ tsp
Tomatoes......................2 large sized	Cinnamon.......................1 inch stick
Fresh coriander leaves.........a few sprigs	Stone flower (dagad phool)..................1
Dry coconut (kopra)..........................½	Cumin seeds.............................½ tsp
Oil...4 tbsps	Bay leaves...................................2
Cloves..8	Black cardamoms.............................2
Peppercorns....................................8	Peppercorns...............................1 tsp
Poppy seeds.............................1 tsp	

Method of preparation

1. Peel, wash carrot and potato and cut into half inch sized cubes.
2. Wash cauliflower florets. String French beans and cut into half inch pieces. Wash and drain green peas.
3. Boil carrot, potato and cauliflower in sufficient quantity of boiling salted water till nearly done and then add French beans and green peas. Boil for five more minutes. Drain and refresh in cold water. Drain again and keep aside.
4. Peel, wash and chop onions. Peel, wash and grind ginger and garlic to a fine paste. Wash and chop tomatoes. Clean, wash and chop coriander leaves. Grate dry coconut.
5. Grind all the ingredients of the Kolhapuri garam masala into a fine powder and keep aside.
6. Heat two tablespoons of oil in a kadai. Add grated dry coconut, cloves, peppercorns, poppy seeds, coriander seeds and whole red chillies. Lightly fry. Now add two-thirds of the chopped onions and cook till it turns slightly brown. Cool, grind to a paste using sufficient water. Keep aside.
7. Heat remaining oil in another kadai. Add the remaining chopped onions and sauté till brown. Add ginger and garlic paste and continue to sauté till lightly browned. Add red chilli powder, turmeric powder, masala paste and half cup of water and cook for two minutes.
8. Add the boiled vegetables, adjust salt and simmer for four to five minutes. Sprinkle Kolhapuri garam masala powder and mix well.
9. Garnish with coriander leaves and serve hot.

Vegetable
Kolhapuri

Paneer Pasanda

Ingredients

Cottage cheese (paneer)	400 gms	Cloves	4 – 5
Green chillies	3	Cinnamon	1 inch stick
Onions	2 large sized	Green cardamoms	4–5
Ginger	1 ½ inch piece	Peppercorns	6–8
Garlic	10 cloves	Red chilli powder	1 tsp
Cashewnuts	10-12	Turmeric powder	¼ tsp
Raisins	15-20	Coriander powder	1 tsp
White pepper powder	½ tsp	Tomato puree	2 cups
Salt	to taste	Green cardamom powder	1 tsp
Cornstarch	½ cup	Sugar	1 tbsp
Oil	2 tbsps + to deep fry	Fresh cream	½ cup
Bay leaf	1		

Method of preparation

1. Mash one-fourth quantity of *paneer* and cut the rest into one and a half inch sized squares with half a centimetre thickness.
2. Remove stems, wash and finely chop green chillies. Peel, wash and cut onions into quarters. Boil in half a cup of water. Drain excess water and grind to a fine paste. Peel and wash ginger. Finely chop half inch piece of ginger. Peel, wash garlic and grind it with the remaining piece of ginger.
3. Soak half the cashewnuts in half a cup of warm water for fifteen minutes. Drain and grind to a paste. Chop the remaining cashewnuts. Wash, pat dry and chop raisins.
4. Mix mashed *paneer* with chopped cashewnuts, raisins, chopped ginger, white pepper powder and season with salt. Mix well and stuff this mixture between two slices of *paneer*.
5. Prepare a thick batter of cornstarch, salt and water. Heat sufficient oil in a *kadai*, dip stuffed *paneer* pieces in the batter and deep fry till crisp and golden. Drain onto an absorbent paper.
6. Heat two tablespoons of oil in another *kadai*. Add bay leaf, cloves, cinnamon, green cardamoms and peppercorns. Add boiled onion paste. Cook for two minutes.
7. Add chopped green chillies, ginger and garlic paste, red chilli powder, turmeric powder and coriander powder. Cook for a minute.
8. Add tomato puree and bring to a boil. Add cashewnut paste dissolved in a little water. Cook for five minutes stirring continuously. Add salt and green cardamom powder.
9. Add one cup of water and sugar. Bring to a boil.
10. Add fried *paneer* pieces and fresh cream and mix. Serve hot.

Ingredients

Chickpeas (kabuli chana)	1 cup	Cumin seeds	1 tsp
Spinach (palak)	2 bunches	Tomato puree	1 cup
Green chillies	3–4	Red chilli powder	1 tsp
Ginger	1 inch piece	Garam masala powder	1 tsp
Garlic	4–5 cloves	Salt	to taste
Ghee	2 tbsps		

Method of preparation

1. Wash and soak chickpeas in four to five cups of water for five to six hours. Drain, add three cups of fresh water and pressure-cook till done. Drain and refresh.
2. Remove stalks, wash and blanch spinach in boiling water for two minutes. Drain, refresh and blend to a puree.
3. Remove stems and wash green chillies. Peel and wash ginger and garlic. Grind the three to a coarse paste using a little water.
4. Heat ghee in a kadai, add cumin seeds and sauté till it changes colour. Add green chilli-ginger-garlic paste and fry for a minute.
5. Add tomato puree, red chilli powder, garam masala powder and salt and fry for a few minutes or till the ghee leaves the masala.
6. Add spinach puree and chickpeas and stir gently. Cover and allow to simmer on low heat for five to six minutes.
7. Serve hot.

Palak Chole

Ingredients

Cottage cheese (paneer)..............200 gms	Salt..................................to taste
Potatoes.........................2 medium sized	White pepper powder....................½ tsp
Green chillies...2	Oil.........................3 tbsps + to deep fry
Ginger..............................½ inch piece	Caraway seeds (shahi jeera)............½ tsp
Raisins......................................12-15	Tomato puree..............................½ cup
Cashewnuts..............................12-15	Turmeric powder............................½ tsp
Spinach (palak)......................2 bunches	Coriander powder............................1 tsp
Garlic..................................5–6 cloves	Garam masala powder....................1 tsp
Cornstarch...............................3 tbsps	Fresh cream.................................¼ cup
Red chilli powder..........................½ tsp	

Method of preparation

1. Mash paneer thoroughly or pass through a sieve. Wash and boil potatoes. Let it cool a little, peel while still warm and mash well. Remove stems, wash and roughly chop green chillies. Peel, wash and finely chop ginger. Wash raisins and pat them dry. Roughly chop raisins and cashewnuts.

2. Clean and wash spinach. Blanch in sufficient amount of boiling water for two to three minutes, refresh in running water and drain well. Grind to a smooth puree along with green chillies. Peel, wash and finely chop garlic.

3. Mix together mashed paneer and potatoes along with cornstarch, red chilli powder, chopped ginger, salt to taste and white pepper powder. Divide the mixture into sixteen even-sized balls. Stuff each ball with chopped cashewnuts and raisins.

4. Heat sufficient oil in a kadai and deep fry the balls a few at a time until golden brown. Drain onto an absorbent paper and keep aside.

5. Heat three tablespoons of oil in a handi, add shahi jeera and garlic and stir-fry. Add spinach puree and cook for about two to three minutes. Stir in tomato puree and mix well.

6. Add turmeric powder, coriander powder and salt. Cook for four to five minutes.

7. Add one cup of water and bring to a boil. Reduce heat and allow to simmer for five to seven minutes. Stir in garam masala powder and cook till curry is reduced to half. Reduce heat, stir in cream and cook for half a minute. Remove from heat.

8. Arrange koftas in a serving dish. Pour hot gravy on top and serve hot.

Paneer
Kofta
in
Spinach
Curry

Ingredients

Cauliflower	1 medium sized	Oil	1 tbsp + to deep fry
Kasoori methi	½ cup	Mustard seeds	½ tsp
Onions	2 medium sized	Coriander powder	1 tbsp
Ginger	1½ inch piece	Turmeric powder	½ tsp
Garlic	10 cloves	Yogurt	½ cup
Green chillies	4	Salt	to taste
Tomatoes	2 medium sized		

Gobhi Kasoori

Method of preparation

1. Wash and cut cauliflower into florets. Keep in salted water for ten minutes. Peel, wash and chop onions. Peel, wash and grind ginger and garlic to a fine paste. Remove stems, wash and chop green chillies. Wash and chop tomatoes.

2. Heat sufficient oil in a *kadai* and deep-fry the cauliflower florets until golden brown. Remove onto an absorbent paper to remove excess oil.

3. Roast *kasoori methi* on a *tawa* on medium heat. Cool slightly and powder.

4. Heat one tablespoon of oil in a pan, add mustard seeds, when they crackle add onions and cook until golden brown in colour. Add green chillies and sauté along with onions.

5. Add ginger and garlic paste, stir for a moment.

6. Add tomatoes and stir. Add half a cup of water, cover and cook.

7. Add coriander powder, turmeric powder and mix. Add yogurt, stir and cook on high heat for five minutes.

8. Add fried cauliflower and mix well. Add salt and *kasoori methi* powder and mix.

9. Cook for five to seven minutes and serve hot.

(See Photo on Page 63)

Ingredients

Tindli............................2 cups (500 gms)	Cumin seeds.....................................¼ tsp
Garlic................................20-24 cloves	Red chillies whole............................4-6
Ginger...................................1 inch piece	Coriander powder.........................1 tbsp
Fresh coriander leaves..........a few sprigs	Turmeric powder..............................1 tsp
Oil...1 tbsp	Salt...to taste

Method of preparation

Lahsooni Tindli

1. Wash tindli and then cut into quarters lengthwise.
2. Peel, wash and pat dry garlic. Peel, wash ginger and grind with ten cloves of garlic to a paste. Clean, wash and chop coriander leaves.
3. Heat oil, add cumin seeds, whole red chillies broken into two and ginger-garlic paste. Cook for a minute.
4. Add remaining garlic cloves and cook for a minute to lightly brown them.
5. Add tindli and cook, stirring continuously, until they are crisp.
6. Add coriander powder, turmeric powder and salt. Mix well.
7. Reduce heat and cook, covered, for five minutes.
8. Remove from heat, garnish with chopped coriander leaves and serve immediately.

Chef's tip: You can use one teaspoon of red chilli powder insted of whole red chillies.

Ingredients

Potatoes..................25-30 medium sized	Asafoetida..............................a pinch
Oil.........................2 tbsps + to deep fry	Fennel seeds (saunf)......................1 tsp
Cottage cheese (paneer)..............100 gms	Cumin seeds...............................1 tsp
Fresh coriander leaves.......1 small bunch	Tomato puree...............................2 cups
Green chillies..................................4-5	Turmeric powder............................½ tsp
Ginger.............................1 inch piece	Red chilli powder..........................½ tsp
Cashewnuts..................................10-15	Tamarind pulp........................1½ tbsps
Jaggery...½ cup	Dry mango powder (amchur).........½ tsp
Raisins...10	Fresh cream................................2 tbsps
Salt...to taste	

Method of preparation

1. Peel, wash and halve potatoes. Heat sufficient oil in a kadai and deep-fry the potatoes till they are golden brown. Drain on an absorbent paper. Let cool and scoop the center of each half potato. Chop scooped out portion of potatoes.

2. Grate paneer. Clean, wash and chop coriander leaves. Remove stems, wash, slit, deseed and chop green chillies. Peel, wash and chop ginger. Chop cashewnuts. Grate jaggery. Wash raisins and pat them dry.

3. In a bowl mix chopped potatoes, paneer, coriander leaves, green chillies, cashewnuts, raisins and salt. Mix well.

4. Stuff scooped out potato halves with this filling and keep aside.

5. Heat two tablespoons of oil in a kadai. Add asafoetida, fennel and cumin seeds and let them change colour. Add ginger and sauté for a minute.

6. Add tomato puree and stir well for two to three minutes. Add turmeric powder, red chilli powder and mix. Add half a cup of water and let it cook for four to five minutes.

7. Add tamarind pulp, amchur, jaggery and salt.

8. Add stuffed potatoes to the gravy and cook on low heat.

9. Add fresh cream and stir gently. Cook till gravy has reduced slightly. Serve hot.

Benarasi
Bharwan
Aloo

Ingredients

Chicken	1 (1 kg)	Salt	to taste
Onions	2 medium sized	Oil	3 tbsps
Ginger	2 one inch pieces	Green cardamoms	4
Garlic	8–10 cloves	Cinnamon	1 inch stick
Fresh coriander leaves	1 medium bunch	Coriander powder	1 tbsp
Fresh mint leaves	1 small bunch	Cumin powder	1 tbsp
Green chillies	6–8	Fresh cream	½ cup
Yogurt	½ cup	Garam masala powder	1 tsp

Method of preparation

Hara Masala Murgh

1. Remove skin, wash and cut chicken into eight pieces on the bone. Peel, wash and finely chop onions.
2. Peel, wash and roughly chop ginger and garlic. Clean, wash and roughly chop coriander and mint leaves. Remove stems and wash green chillies. Slit two green chillies and reserve for tempering. Grind ginger, garlic, coriander leaves, mint leaves, remaining green chillies to a fine paste along with yogurt. Add salt to taste and mix well.
3. Marinate chicken pieces in this paste for an hour, preferably in a refrigerator.
4. Heat oil in a *kadai*, add green cardamoms, cinnamon and slit green chillies and sauté for a minute. Add onions and sauté till pink.
5. Add coriander and cumin powders and fry for a minute.
6. Add the chicken with the marinade and sauté on medium heat for two minutes. Cover and cook on medium heat for ten to fifteen minutes or till done adding a cup of chicken stock or water if required.
7. Adjust seasoning, stir in the fresh cream and *garam masala* powder. Simmer for two minutes.
8. Serve hot.

Ingredients

Chicken....................................1 (800 gms)	Red chilli powder........................1½ tsps
Green chillies.....................................4-5	Salt..to taste
Fresh coriander leaves.........a few sprigs	Butter..3 tbsps
Ginger.........................2 one inch pieces	Lemon juice.......................................1 tbsp
Garlic...6–8	Fresh cream..½ cup
Tomatoes...................... 6 medium sized	Coal.................................2 large pieces
Cashewnuts...................................10–15	Ghee..1 tbsp
Garam masala powder...................1 tsp	

Koyla Chicken

Method of preparation

1. Remove skin, wash and cut chicken into eight pieces on the bone. Remove stems, wash and slit green chillies. Clean, wash and finely chop coriander leaves. Peel, wash and grind ginger and garlic to a fine paste.
2. Wash and blanch tomatoes in boiling water for two to three minutes. Drain. Peel the tomatoes and puree them in a blender.
3. Dry roast cashewnuts and coarsely grind with a mortar and pestle.
4. Marinate the chicken pieces in ginger and garlic paste, garam masala powder, red chilli powder and salt for an hour preferably in a refrigerator.
5. Heat butter in a kadai. Add the marinated chicken and sauté for two minutes. Add slit green chillies and continue to sauté for a minute.
6. Add tomato puree and half a cup of water and cover and cook on medium heat for fifteen minutes or till almost done.
7. Add crushed cashewnuts and cover and simmer for three to four minutes or till chicken is tender.
8. Add lemon juice and coriander leaves and cook for a minute or till oil leaves the masala. Stir in the fresh cream and mix gently. Remove from heat.
9. Place coal on an open flame and heat till it becomes red hot. Remove from heat and put the coal in a small steel bowl, place the bowl over the chicken, pour a tablespoon of warm ghee over the coal. As soon as it begins to smoke, cover the kadai with a lid. Open the lid after ten minutes, remove bowl with coal and serve hot.

Ingredients

Chicken.....................1 (800 gms)	Cashewnuts.....................10–15
Fresh fenugreek leaves (methi)...............	Salt.....................to taste
.....................2 small bunches	Ghee.....................3 tbsps
Onions.....................2 medium sized	Caraway seeds (shahi jeera).............1 tsp
Ginger.....................1 inch piece	Cinnamon.....................1 inch stick
Garlic.....................4–5 cloves	Cloves.....................4–5
Green chillies.....................4	Peppercorns.....................6–8
Yogurt.....................¾ cup	Fresh cream (malai).....................¾ cup

Method of preparation

Murgh
Methi
Malai

1. Wash, remove skin and cut chicken into eight pieces on the bone. Clean, wash and blanch *methi* leaves in boiling water for two minutes. Drain, refresh and chop finely.

2. Peel, wash and roughly chop onions, ginger and garlic. Remove stems, wash and roughly chop green chillies. Grind them all to a fine paste.

3. Whisk yogurt till smooth. Soak cashewnuts in half a cup of water for fifteen minutes and grind to a fine paste.

4. Mix together yogurt, the onion-ginger-garlic-green chilli paste and salt. Marinate the chicken pieces in this mixture for half an hour, preferably in a refrigerator.

5. Heat one tablespoon of *ghee* in a pan, add *shahi jeera*. When they change colour add *methi* leaves and salt to taste and sauté on medium heat for two minutes. Remove from heat and keep aside.

6. Heat two tablespoons of *ghee* in a *kadai*, add cinnamon, cloves and peppercorns and allow to crackle. Add the chicken with the marinade and mix. Add cashewnut paste with half a cup of water. Bring to a boil. Reduce heat, cover and cook for twelve to fifteen minutes or till chicken is almost done adding very little water, if required, to avoid scorching.

7. Add sautéed *methi* leaves and continue to cook for two to three minutes or till the chicken is done.

8. Gently stir in the cream. Serve hot.

Ingredients

Chicken	1 (800 gms)	Poppy seeds (khuskhus)	6 tbsps
Onions	4 medium sized	Oil	4 tbsps
Ginger	½ inch piece	Coriander seeds	2 tsps
Garlic	10 cloves	Cumin seeds	1 tsp
Fresh coriander leaves	a few sprigs	Red chilli powder	1 tsp
Gongura leaves	20–25	Garam masala powder	1½ tsps
Green chillies	5	Salt	to taste

Method of preparation

1. Wash, clean, remove skin and cut chicken into eight pieces. Peel, wash and chop onions. Peel and wash ginger and garlic. Grind half the garlic with ginger into a fine paste. Chop the remaining garlic cloves. Clean, wash and finely chop fresh coriander leaves.

2. Wash *gongura* leaves, drain well and roughly chop them. Remove stems, wash green chillies and break into two. Soak *khuskhus* in one-fourth cup of water for half an hour and then grind into a fine paste.

3. Heat two tablespoons of oil in a pan and stir-fry chopped garlic, *gongura* leaves and green chillies. Keep aside. Roast coriander seeds on a griddle. Cool and crush coarsely in a mortar.

4. Heat remaining oil in a pan, add cumin seeds, sauté till they change colour. Add onions and fry till golden brown. Add ginger and garlic paste. Sauté for a minute. Add red chilli powder, *khuskhus* paste, *garam masala* powder and crushed coriander seeds.

5. Add chicken and sauté for three to four minutes. Add two cups of water and salt. Cook covered for five minutes.

6. Add *gongura* leaves fried with garlic and green chillies. Stir and cook, uncovered, for another ten to twelve minutes or till the chicken is cooked.

7. Serve hot garnished with fresh coriander leaves.

Gongura Chicken

Ingredients

Chicken (breasts)......................................8	Kewra water.....................................1 tsp
Lemon juice................................3½ tbsps	Fennel powder..............................¼ tsp
White pepper powder......................½ tsp	Green cardamom powder............a pinch
Salt..to taste	Oil...2 tbsps
Ginger..........................2 one inch pieces	Cinnamon......................2 one inch sticks
Garlic.......................................6-8 cloves	Cloves...4-5
Green apple.................1 medium sized	Green cardamoms..........................3-4
Curry leaves..................................6-8	Cumin seeds..................................½ tsp
Chicken liver....................................4	Madras curry powder...................2 tsps
Chicken mince.............................1 cup	Turmeric powder..........................½ tsp
Prawns.........................6 medium sized	Tomato puree................................1 cup
Egg...1	Fresh cream.................................½ cup
Saffron.............................10-12 strands	Green peppercorns...........................8-10

Murgh Jugalbandi

Method of preparation

1. Clean, wash and split open chicken breasts. Sprinkle two tablespoons of lemon juice, white pepper powder and salt. Rub lightly on the chicken breast and set aside for about ten minutes, preferably in a refrigerator.

2. Peel and wash ginger and garlic. Grind half the ginger and garlic to a fine paste. Chop the remaining ginger finely. Peel the green apple and slice finely. Sprinkle half a tablespoon of lemon juice to avoid discolouration. Wash curry leaves and pat them dry. Clean, wash and boil chicken liver. Cut into one centimeter sized cubes. Clean, wash and completely drain chicken mince.

4. Peel, de-vein and wash prawns thoroughly. Cut into one centimetre-sized pieces. Beat egg and keep aside. Dissolve saffron in kewra water.

5. Take chicken mince in a bowl and add chopped ginger, fennel powder, green cardamom powder, chopped liver, chopped prawns, half the beaten egg, salt and mix thoroughly. Brush chicken breasts with little of the remaining beaten egg.

6. Place a tablespoon of the chicken mince on one corner and roll into cornets. Grill the chicken cornets lightly on a hot plate or a non-stick pan using a tablespoon of oil, turning regularly for even colouring and cooking.

7. Heat the remaining oil, add cinnamon, cloves, green cardamoms and cumin seeds, stir-fry for a few seconds. Add curry leaves and immediately add ginger and garlic paste. Stir-fry for ten to fifteen seconds. Add green apple and stir-fry until the apple softens.

8. Add the Madras curry powder, turmeric powder and stir-fry. Add tomato puree and simmer the gravy for about eight to ten minutes. Remove and strain. If the gravy is thick add half a cup of water.

9. Heat the strained gravy and add the grilled cornets. Simmer for about two to three minutes. Add remaining lemon juice and saffron dissolved in kewra water. Simmer for another minute and stir in cream. Add green peppercorns and mix. Remove from heat and serve hot.

Ingredients

Chicken (boneless).....................500 gms	Red chilli powder........................1½ tsps
Onions.........................3 medium sized	Salt..to taste
Capsicum........................1 medium sized	Oil..5 tbsps
Ginger................1 inch + 1½ inch pieces	Cumin seeds...............................1½ tsps
Garlic...10 cloves	Red chillies whole.................................3
Fresh coriander leaves.........a few sprigs	Tomato puree................................½ cup
Vinegar...2 tbsps	Tomato ketchup...........................2 tbsps

Method of preparation

1. Wash, pat dry chicken and cut into thin strips.
2. Peel, wash and slice onions thinly. Wash, halve, deseed and cut capsicum into thin strips. Peel, wash and cut one inch piece of ginger into julienne. Peel and wash the remaining piece of ginger. Peel and wash garlic. Grind ginger and garlic to a smooth paste. Clean, wash and chop fresh coriander leaves.
3. Marinate the chicken strips in one tablespoon of vinegar, half the red chilli powder, half the ginger-garlic paste and salt to taste for half an hour, preferably in a refrigerator.
4. Heat oil in a deep pan. Add cumin seeds and whole red chillies. Stir-fry till the cumin seeds change colour. Add the sliced onions and stir fry till translucent. Add the remaining ginger- garlic paste and sauté for two to three minutes.
5. Add the marinated chicken and stir-fry for three to four minutes. Add tomato puree, tomato ketchup, remaining red chilli powder and stir fry till the chicken is almost dry. Adjust the seasoning.
6. Add ginger julienne, capsicum strips, chopped coriander leaves, remaining vinegar and toss.
7. Serve hot.

Chicken Jalfraezi

71

Ingredients

Chicken	1 (1 kg)	Cumin seeds	1 tsp
Onions	2 medium sized	Cloves	6
Oil	3 tbsps + to deep fry	Green cardamoms	8
Green chillies	6	Peppercorns	8
Ginger	1 inch piece	Cinnamon	1 inch stick
Garlic	4-5 cloves	Salt	to taste
Coriander seeds	1 tbsp	Vinegar	3 tbsps

Method of preparation

1. Wash, remove skin, trim and cut chicken into eight medium sized pieces. Make deep incisions on the chicken using a sharp knife.
2. Peel, wash and finely slice onions. Heat sufficient oil in a kadai and deep fry onions till crisp and golden brown. Drain onto an absorbent paper and reserve for garnish.
3. Remove stems and wash green chillies. Peel and wash ginger and garlic.
4. Dry roast coriander seeds, cumin seeds, cloves, green cardamoms, peppercorns and cinnamon. Grind ginger, garlic, green chillies and roasted masala to a paste using a little water.
5. Add salt to the paste and apply this paste to the chicken and refrigerate for two to three hours.
6. Heat three tablespoons of oil in a pan, add the marinated chicken and cook, covered on medium heat, stirring occasionally. Add a little warm water if required to avoid scorching. Cook for eight to ten minutes.
7. When almost done add vinegar and simmer for two to three minutes.
8. Serve hot garnished with fried onions.

Chef's tip: If you like you can add a little fresh coriander to the paste. I know of a Goan restaurant which does it and it tastes delicious.

Chicken
Cafreal

Ingredients

Mutton	500 gms	Coriander seeds	2 tsps
Onions	4 medium sized	Cloves	4-5
Ginger	2 one inch pieces	Peppercorns	½ tsp
Garlic	10 cloves	Cumin seeds	½ tsp
Fresh coriander leaves	a few sprigs	Caraway seeds (shahi jeera)	½ tsp
Oil	4 tbsps	Green cardamoms	4-5
Salt	to taste	Black cardamoms	2-3
Turmeric powder	½ tsp	Dry coconut (grated)	½ cup
For malvani masala		Poppy seeds (khuskhus)	1 tsp
Red chillies whole	10		

Method of preparation

1. Clean, wash and cut mutton into one-inch sized cubes.
2. Peel, wash and slice onions finely. Peel, wash and cut one piece of ginger into julienne. Peel, wash the remaining ginger and garlic and grind to a fine paste. Clean, wash and chop coriander leaves finely.
3. For malvani masala remove stems of red chillies. Roast on a hot griddle.
4. Dry roast coriander seeds, cloves, peppercorns, cumin seeds, caraway seeds, green cardamoms, black cardamoms, grated dry coconut and poppy seeds separately.
5. Mix all the roasted ingredients and grind to a fine paste with a little water.
6. Heat oil in a thick-bottomed vessel, add the onions, sauté till light golden brown.
7. Add the ginger and garlic paste, sauté for a few seconds.
8. Add the mutton pieces, sauté for a few minutes, add four cups of water and salt to taste and let it cook, covered, on low heat.
9. Once the mutton is cooked, add the ground masala, turmeric powder and mix well. If the gravy is too thick add another half a cup of water and simmer for two to three minutes.
10. Check the seasoning. Serve hot, garnished with coriander leaves and ginger julienne.

Malvani Mutton

Mangshor Jhol

Ingredients

Mutton pieces	½ kg	Red chilli powder	1½ tsps
Potatoes	2 medium sized	Turmeric powder	½ tsp
Onions	2 large sized	Coriander powder	1 tsp
Ginger	½ inch piece	Cumin powder	1 tsp
Garlic	5 cloves	Oil	to deep fry
Fresh coriander leaves	a few sprigs	Desi ghee	2 tbsps
Yogurt	½ cup	Bay leaves	2
Salt	to taste	Paanch phoron	1 tsp
Mustard oil	2 tbsps	Garam masala powder	½ tsp

Method of preparation

1. Wash and trim mutton pieces. Peel, wash and cut potatoes into one inch sized cubes and keep them in a bowl of water to avoid discolouration. Peel, wash and finely slice onions. Peel, wash and grind ginger and garlic to a fine paste. Clean, wash and finely chop coriander leaves. Whisk yogurt till smooth.

2. In a large bowl combine the mutton, yogurt, salt, ginger and garlic paste, mustard oil, red chilli powder, turmeric powder, coriander powder and cumin powder and allow to marinate for two hours, preferably in a refrigerator.

3. Heat sufficient oil in a kadai and deep fry potatoes till golden brown. Drain onto an absorbent paper.

4. Heat desi ghee in a kadai, add bay leaves and paanch phoron and allow to splutter. Add onions and fry till brown.

5. Add mutton with the marinade and three cups of water. Bring to a boil. Reduce heat, cover and allow to simmer on low heat, stirring occasionally for forty to forty-five minutes.

6. When the mutton is tender, add garam masala powder, potatoes and coriander leaves. Stir and serve hot.

7. Alternatively you can cook the dish in a pressure cooker with two cups of water and reduce the cooking time accordingly.

Note: Paanch Phoron is a mixture of equal quantities of cumin seeds, mustard seeds, fenugreek seeds, fennel seeds and onion seeds.

(See Photo on Page 74)

Ingredients

Lamb (boneless)........................600 gms	Peppercorns (crushed)....................1 tsp
Onions...........................5 medium sized	Cloves..2
Oil........................4 tbsps + to deep fry	Green cardamoms..2
Yogurt.......................................1¼ cups	Peppercorns..5
Ginger..............................1 inch piece	Cinnamon..........................½ inch stick
Garlic...............................10 cloves	Bay leaf...1
Green chillies................................4–5	Coriander powder........................1 tbsp
Cashewnuts..................................10–12	Garam masala powder..................½ tsp
Salt..to taste	Green cardamom powder................1 tsp

Method of preparation

1. Clean, wash and cut lamb into one-and-a-half inch sized cubes. Flatten them by using a steak hammer.
2. Peel, wash and thinly slice onions. Heat sufficient oil in a kadai and deep fry onions. Drain onto an absorbent paper. Grind the fried onions with half a cup of yogurt to a fine paste.
3. Peel, wash and grind ginger and garlic into a fine paste. Remove stems, wash and slit green chillies.
4. Soak cashewnuts in water for half an hour and then make a paste using one-fourth cup of yogurt.
5. Marinate flattened lamb pieces in the remaining yogurt, salt, ginger and garlic paste, crushed peppercorns for about two hours, preferably in a refrigerator.
6. Heat four tablespoons of oil in a thick-bottomed pan. Add cloves, green cardamoms, peppercorns, cinnamon and bay leaf and sauté for a minute.
7. Add marinated lamb pieces and stir-fry on high heat for five to six minutes. Reduce heat and add slit green chillies, coriander powder and stir for one to two minutes. Add one and a half cups of water and continue to cook, covered, on medium heat, for ten minutes.
8. Add cashewnut and yogurt paste and cook for seven to eight minutes.
9. Now add brown onion paste and mix well. Cook till mutton is fully cooked.
10. Sprinkle garam masala powder and green cardamom powder. Stir and serve hot.

Gosht Pasanda

Ingredients

Mutton (leg)......................................1 kg		Turmeric powder............................¼ tsp	
Onions...........................4 medium sized		Salt...to taste	
Garlic......................................10 cloves		Desi ghee..½ cup	
Fresh coriander leaves..........a few sprigs		Bay leaves...1	
Red chillies whole..........................15-20		Black cardamoms...................................2	
Cumin seeds.................................¾ tsp		Green cardamoms...................................4	
Coriander seeds...........................2 tbsps		Cinnamon.....................2 one inch sticks	
Yogurt..1 cup			

Method of preparation

1. Clean, wash and cut mutton into one-inch sized cubes.
2. Peel, wash and slice the onions and garlic. Clean, wash and chop the coriander leaves.
3. Remove stems, de-seed red chillies and crush lightly. Dry roast cumin and coriander seeds on a griddle. Cool and grind to a powder.
4. Mix together yogurt, red chillies, cumin and coriander powder, turmeric powder and salt. Add mutton and allow to marinate for half an hour preferably in a refrigerator.
5. Heat desi ghee in a pan, add bay leaves, black and green cardamoms, cinnamon, garlic and sauté till light golden. Add onions and continue to sauté till the onions too turn golden.
6. Add the mutton pieces along with the marinade and sauté for another four to five minutes.
7. Add three cups of water and bring to boil. Cover tightly and simmer till the mutton is cooked and tender. Stir occasionally. Adjust seasoning.
8. Garnish with coriander leaves and serve hot.

Lal Maas

Ingredients

Mutton (boneless).....................500 gms	Oil...2 tbsps
Onion............................1 medium sized	Cumin seeds................................1 tsp
Green chillies.....................................5	Milk ....½ cup
Fresh coriander leaves.........a few sprigs	White pepper powder...................½ tsp
Ginger............................½ inch piece	Fresh cream...............................4 tbsps
Garlic...................................5 cloves	Green cardamom powder................1 tsp
Cashewnuts...................................20-25	Kewra water..............................3 drops
Eggs...3	Desi ghee...................................3 tbsps
Salt..to taste	

Method of preparation

1. Clean, wash and cut mutton into one inch sized pieces. Peel, wash and chop onion finely. Remove stems, wash and chop green chillies finely. Wash, clean and chop coriander leaves finely. Peel, wash and grind ginger and garlic to a fine paste.

2. Soak cashewnuts in one cup of water for half an hour. Blend to a fine paste. Beat eggs with salt.

3. Heat oil in a *kadai*, add cumin seeds. Sauté till they change colour. Add onions and sauté till transparent. Add ginger-garlic paste and sauté for a minute. Add mutton, sauté for three to four minutes without allowing it to brown. Add milk and one cup of water. Cover and cook for twenty to twenty-five minutes or till the mutton is three-fourth cooked.

4. Add cashewnut paste, salt and white pepper powder. Stir for five to seven minutes on medium heat, till the gravy starts simmering and becomes thick. Add cream, green cardamom powder and *kewra* water.

5. Remove from heat. Transfer into a *handi* with a narrow opening.

6. Preheat an oven to 160°C.

7. Heat *desi ghee*. Put some beaten egg on the mutton and pour the hot *desi ghee* on top. Repeat this process till all the beaten egg is used up to seal the mutton.

8. Cook in a preheated moderate oven at 160° C for fifteen to twenty minutes.

9. Garnish with coriander leaves and serve hot.

Ingredients

Prawns	20-25 small sized	Coconut	½
Tender coconuts (daab)	2	Mustard paste	2 tbsps
Onions	2 medium sized	Salt	to taste
Ginger	1½ inch piece	Mustard oil	2 tbsps
Garlic	15 cloves	Paanch phoron	1 tsp
Green chillies	4–6	Refined flour (maida) dough	as required

Method of preparation

Daab Chingri

1. Shell, de-vein and wash prawns. Chop into small pieces.
2. Take tender coconuts, cut off an inch from the tops and remove water, retain the tops to act as lids.
3. Peel, wash and halve onions. Slice them lengthwise very finely. Peel, wash and grind ginger and garlic to a fine paste. Remove stems, wash and slit green chillies. Scrape the coconut.
4. Preheat oven to 220°C.
5. In a bowl mix prawns, onions, ginger and garlic paste, green chillies, scraped coconut, mustard paste and salt to taste.
6. Stuff the tender coconuts with the above mixture.
7. Heat mustard oil in a pan. Add paanch phoron and when it crackles, pour it into the tender coconuts.
8. Cover the tender coconuts using the top slices. Seal the tops with the maida dough.
9. Bake at 220°C for approximately forty-five minutes in which time the prawns should be cooked and mustard oil should have risen to the top of the shells.
10. Remove the lids at the table while serving the dish.

Note: Paanch phoron is a mixture of equal quantities of mustard seeds, cumin seeds, fenugreek seeds, fennel seeds and onion seeds.

Ingredients

Prawns (small)	25-30	Fenugreek seeds	1 tsp
Turmeric powder	1 tsp	Fresh coconut (scraped)	2 cups
Salt	to taste	Oil	6 tbsps
Sambar onions	9-10	Red chilli powder	1 tbsp
Green chillies	6	Coriander powder	1 tbsp
Curd chillies	4-6	Kodumpuli	6 pieces
Drumsticks	2	Red chillies whole	4
Raw mango	1 medium sized	Coconut oil	1 tbsp
Curry leaves	2 sprigs		

Method of preparation

1. Shell, de-vein and wash the prawns. Pat them dry and marinate in half a teaspoon of turmeric powder and little salt.

2. Peel and wash onions. Remove stems, wash and slit green chillies and curd chillies.

3. Wash, string and cut drumsticks into one-inch length pieces. Wash, peel mango and cut into wedges. Wash curry leaves and pat them dry.

4. Lightly pound the fenugreek seeds. Soak and grind coconut with one cup of warm water and extract a thick milk and keep aside. Keep the coconut residue also.

5. Heat four tablespoons of oil in a vessel, add onions and fry till transparent. Add red chilli powder, remaining turmeric powder, coriander powder and stir.

6. Put in the green chillies and curd chillies, curry leaves and kodumpuli. Add coconut residue and four cups of water. Boil till it reduces to half and thickens. Keep aside.

7. Heat remaining oil and coconut oil in a pan, add the pounded fenugreek methi seeds and whole red chillies and stir well.

8. Add the marinated prawns, drumsticks and mango. Cook till prawns are three-fourths done.

9. Pour in the curry and simmer till it combines well. Add salt to taste.

10. Remove from heat and add the coconut milk and let simmer for five minutes. Serve hot.

Chef's tip: Traditionally this curry is made in a clay pot. Tastes excellent with steamed rice and so keep the curry a little thin in consistency. You can use any kind of fish or seafood and prepare this curry.

Note: Curd chillies: Chillies are soaked in a mixture of thin curd and salt for 6-8 hours and then sun-dried till all the moisture dries up. They are then stored in airtight tins to use when required. They can be deep-fried and used as an accompaniment also.

Malabar Chemeen Kari

81

Prawn Ghassi

Ingredients

Prawns	18-20 medium sized	Coriander seeds	2 tsps
Salt	to taste	Cumin seeds	1 tsp
Onions	2 medium sized	Peppercorns	8 – 10
Garlic	5 cloves	Fenugreek seeds	¼ tsp
Fresh coriander leaves	a few sprigs	Turmeric powder	½ tsp
Red chillies whole	4	Tamarind pulp	1½ tbsps
Coconut (scraped)	1 cup	Oil	3 tbsps

Method of preparation

1. Remove shells, de-vein and wash prawns thoroughly under running water. Drain and pat them dry. Sprinkle salt and marinate for one hour preferably in the refrigerator.
2. Peel, wash and finely chop one onion and roughly chop the other. Peel and wash garlic cloves. Clean, wash and chop coriander leaves. Dry roast whole red chillies.
3. Grind scraped coconut, roughly chopped onion, whole red chillies, coriander seeds, cumin seeds, peppercorns, fenugreek seeds, turmeric powder, garlic and tamarind pulp to a smooth paste using sufficient water and keep aside.
4. Heat oil in a kadai and fry chopped onions till light brown.
5. Add ground masala paste and sauté for two to three minutes. Add two cups of water and mix well. When the water comes to a boil add prawns and adjust seasoning.
6. Simmer for five minutes or till cooked and serve hot garnished with chopped coriander leaves.

Ingredients

Pomfrets......................2 (500 gms. each)	Cumin seeds.....................................½ tsp
Salt......................................to taste	Garlic..8 cloves
Lemon juice.................................1 tbsp	Peppercorns...................................5–6
Turmeric powder.........................¼ tsp	Ginger..................................1 inch piece
Oil.......................to shallow fry	Cloves..4–5
Lemons...2	Cinnamon...........................½ inch stick
Onion..........................1 medium sized	Vinegar.......................................2 tbsps
For the masala paste	Sugar..½ tsp
Red chillies whole...............................8	Salt..to taste

Method of preparation

1. Wash, clean and pat dry the fish. Make diagonal slits on either sides of the fish using a sharp knife. Rub salt, lemon juice, turmeric powder inside and outside of the fish. Keep aside for half an hour preferably in the refrigerator.
2. Combine all the ingredients of the masala and grind to a smooth paste, using little water if required.
3. Apply the paste on both the sides of the fish and keep aside for fifteen minutes preferably in the refrigerator.
4. Wash and cut lemons into wedges. Peel, wash and cut onion into roundels and then separate into rings. Keep aside to serve as accompaniments.
5. Heat oil in a pan and shallow fry the fish till golden on both sides.
6. Serve hot with lemon wedges, onion rings and chutney of your choice.

Pomfret
Recheiado

Narangi Pulao

Ingredients

Rice	1½ cups	Cinnamon	2 one-inch sticks
Oranges	6-8 medium sized	Cloves	2
Peppercorns	7-8	Green cardamoms	2
Saffron	few strands	Sea-salt	to taste
Milk	1 tbsp	Sugar	¼ cup
Desi ghee	¼ cup		

Method of preparation

1. Cut oranges into two halves. Extract juice and keep the eight halves for service. Use skin of two oranges to cut into julienne. Boil orange rind julienne in water for a minute, drain and keep aside.
2. Crush peppercorns coarsely. Dissolve saffron in milk.
3. Pick rice. Wash twice and soak in four cups of water for half an hour. Drain and keep aside.
4. Heat *desi ghee* in a saucepan. Add cinnamon, cloves, green cardamoms and sauté for a minute. Add rice and sauté.
5. Add two cups of orange juice and one cup of water to the rice.
6. Add sea-salt, sugar, freshly crushed peppercorns and orange rind and stir once.
7. Add dissolved saffron and stir once. Cover tightly and cook on medium heat till done.
8. Serve rice in orange halves.

Ingredients

Basmati rice	1½ cups	Oil	4 tbsps
Chicken mince	200 gms	Cloves	2
Onions	3 medium sized	Cinnamon	½ inch stick
Ginger	1½ inch piece	Green cardamoms	2
Garlic	10-12 cloves	Peppercorns	8-10
Green chillies	3–4	Cumin seeds	1 tsp
Tomatoes	2 medium sized	Red chilli powder	1 tsp
Fresh mint leaves	15–20	Salt	to taste
Fresh coriander leaves	a few sprigs	Garam masala powder	½ tsp

Method of preparation

1. Pick basmati rice. Wash twice and soak in three cups of water for half an hour. Drain and keep aside. Wash chicken mince, drain and keep aside.
2. Peel, wash and slice onions. Peel, wash and grind ginger and garlic to a fine paste. Remove stems, wash and slit green chillies. Wash and chop tomatoes. Clean, wash and tear mint leaves. Clean, wash and finely chop coriander leaves.
3. Heat oil in a pan, add cloves, cinnamon, green cardamoms, peppercorns, cumin seeds, onion and green chillies. Sauté till the onions begin to change colour.
4. Add chicken mince and cook on high heat for four to five minutes.
5. Add ginger and garlic paste, red chilli powder, tomatoes, three cups of hot water, salt and basmati rice. Mix lightly.
6. Allow rice to come to a boil on high heat. Cover the pan and cook on low heat for twelve to fifteen minutes.
7. Add mint leaves, coriander leaves and garam masala powder. Cover and further cook for five to seven minutes.
8. Remove from heat and serve hot.

Chicken
Kheema Pulao

Ingredients

Chicken	½ kg	Saffron	a generous pinch
Basmati rice	1½ cups	Kewra water	½ tsp
Onions	4 medium sized	Yogurt	½ cup
Ginger	1 inch piece	Ghee	4 tbsps + for deep frying
Garlic	5 cloves	Almonds	10
Green cardamoms	6	Red chilli powder	1½ tsps
Cloves	6	Salt	to taste
Black cardamoms	6	Bay leaves	2
Mace	2 blades	Dough (made of atta)	
Cinnamon	2 one inch sticks		to seal the handi

Lucknowi Murgh Biryani

Method of preparation

1. Clean, wash and cut chicken into small pieces, keep aside. Wash and soak rice in three cups of water for one hour. Drain and keep aside.

2. Peel, wash and finely slice onions. Peel, wash and grind ginger and garlic to a fine paste. Grind half the quantities of green cardamoms, cloves, black cardamoms, mace and cinnamon. Dissolve saffron in kewra water. Whisk yogurt and keep aside.

3. In a kadai heat sufficient ghee and deep-fry the onions till golden brown. Drain onto an absorbent paper.

4. In a deep pan heat one and a half tablespoons of ghee. Add ginger and garlic paste and sauté for two to three minutes. Add red chilli powder, salt, ground masala and continue to sauté till ghee separates. Add chicken pieces, yogurt and sauté for five to seven minutes more.

5. Add three cups of water and cook on a low heat till the chicken is tender. Remove from heat and strain the chicken stock through a strainer.

6. Separate the chicken pieces and stir-fry in a tablespoon of ghee on low heat till slightly crisp on both the sides.

7. Heat remaining one and a half tablespoons of ghee in a deep pan or handi, add bay leaves and the remaining green cardamoms, cloves, black cardamoms, mace, cinnamon. Sauté for two minutes, add drained rice and sauté on medium heat for five minutes.

8. Remove half the quantity of rice. Layer the cooked chicken pieces and almonds over the rice remaining in the pan and top it with the rice that was removed from the pan. Sprinkle kewra water and saffron mixture. Pour the chicken stock on it, cover and seal with the dough. Cook on dum for thirty minutes.

9. Remove and serve hot garnished with fried onions.

Chef's tip: These days ready Biryani Masala is easily available in the market which gives equally good results.

Ingredients

Mutton or lamb....................1 kg	Green cardamoms.....................5
Basmati rice....................2 cups	Black cardamom.....................1
Ginger........................2 two inch pieces	Peppercorns.....................10
Garlic....................20–25 cloves	Potli masala.....................¼ cup
Green chillies.....................2	Caraway seeds (shahi jeera)............½ tsp
Onions....................4-5 large sized	Cardamom powder.....................½ tsp
Fresh coriander leaves.......1 small bunch	Garam masala powder.................2 tsps
Fresh mint leaves.............1 small bunch	Ghee....................5 tbsps
Oil....................to deep fry	Saffron....................a few strands
Yogurt....................2 cups	Milk....................3 tbsps
Red chilli powder....................2 tsps	Rose petals.....................2 tbsps
Turmeric powder....................1 tsp	Rose water.....................1 tsp
Salt....................to taste	Kewra water.....................1 tsp
Cloves....................5-6	Dough (made of atta).................to seal
Cinnamon....................1 inch stick	

Method of preparation

1. Clean, wash and cut mutton into two inch sized pieces. Pick, wash and soak rice in four cups of water for half an hour. Drain and keep aside. Peel and wash ginger and garlic. Grind half the ginger and garlic to a fine paste. Cut the remaining ginger into julienne. Remove stems, wash and chop green chillies. Peel, wash and slice onions finely.

2. Clean, wash and chop coriander leaves. Clean, wash and chop half the mint leaves.

3. Heat sufficient oil in a kadai and deep-fry the onion slices till brown and crisp. Drain onto an absorbent paper and set aside.

4. Take the mutton pieces in a bowl. Add yogurt, ginger and garlic paste, chopped green chillies, red chilli powder, turmeric powder, salt, one-third of the fried sliced onions and chopped mint leaves and mix.

5. Boil five cups of water in another pan to cook the rice. Put cloves, cinnamon, green cardamoms, black cardamoms, peppercorns and potli masala in a muslin cloth and tie up in a potli. Add this potli to the boiling water. Add salt, caraway seeds and the soaked rice. Bring to a boil and cook till partly done. Drain.

6. In a thick bottomed vessel arrange half of the marinated mutton. Over it

Kachche Gosht Ki Biryani

arrange half of the parboiled rice. Then arrange one-third of the fried sliced onions and ginger julienne. Sprinkle half of the cardamom powder, garam masala powder and chopped coriander leaves. Tear half the remaining mint leaves and spread. Pour half *ghee* on top.

7. Warm milk slightly and dissolve saffron in it. Add half the saffron milk to the pan. Sprinkle half of the rose petals, rose water and *kewra* water.

8. Repeat the layers once again. Cover the vessel with a lid. Seal the lid with flour dough. Cook on high heat for five minutes then lower the heat. Keep on a *tawa* and cook on low heat for forty-five minutes. Serve hot with a *raita* of your choice.

Ingredients

Rice	1½ cups	Green peas	¾ cup
Prawns	20-25 small sized	Desi ghee	5 tbsps
Red chilli powder	1¼ tsps	Paanch phoron	½ tsp
Turmeric powder	½ tsp	Cloves	4-5
Onions	2 medium sized	Peppercorns	6-8
Garlic	5 cloves	Cinnamon	1 inch stick
Ginger	¾ inch piece	Mustard paste	½ tsp
Green chillies	3	Coconut milk	¾ cup
Tomatoes	2 small sized	Salt	to taste
Fresh coriander leaves	a few sprigs	Lemon juice	1½ tbsps

Chingri Macher Pulao

Method of preparation

1. Pick rice. Wash twice and soak in three cups of water for thirty minutes. Drain and keep aside.

2. Clean, de-vein the prawns and wash thoroughly under running water. Apply red chilli powder, turmeric powder and keep aside for half an hour, preferably in a refrigerator.

3. Peel, wash and finely chop onion, garlic and ginger. Remove stems, wash and slit green chillies. Wash, halve, de-seed and quarter tomatoes. Clean, wash and chop coriander leaves. Wash and drain green peas.

4. Heat three tablespoons of *ghee* in a large saucepan and fry the onion, garlic, ginger and slit green chillies till light brown.

5. Add *paanch phoron*, cloves, peppercorns, cinnamon and mustard paste. Fry for half a minute.

6. Add rice and fry for two to three minutes.

7. Add two and a quarter cups of water, three-fourth cup of coconut milk and salt to taste. Bring to a boil, cover and cook over low heat.

8. In another saucepan heat the remaining *ghee* and fry the prawns and peas for two to three minutes.

9. When the rice is nearly done, add prawns and peas mixture, stir very gently, cover and cook till done.

10. Sprinkle lemon juice and mix lightly. Serve hot garnished with tomato quarters and chopped coriander leaves.

Note: Paanch phoron is a mixture of equal quantities of mustard seeds, cumin seeds, fenugreek seeds, fennel seeds and onion seeds.

Ingredients

Refined flour (maida)	2 cups	Almonds	10
Baking powder	½ tsp	Raisins (optional)	12-14
Salt	to taste	Sunflower seeds (chironji)	1 tbsp
Milk	¾ cup	Kewra water	1 tsp
Sugar	2½ tsps	Desi ghee	5 tbsps
Fresh yeast	1 tbsp		

Method of preparation

1. Sieve refined flour with baking powder and salt. Heat milk and dissolve sugar in it. Dissolve fresh yeast in a quarter cup of warm water and keep aside.
2. Soak almonds in half a cup of hot water for five minutes, drain, peel and finely slice. Soak raisins and *chironji* in half a cup of warm water for five minutes, drain and keep aside.
3. Make a well in the centre of the sieved flour, add milk, few drops of *kewra* water and dissolved yeast and gradually mix in to make a soft dough. Cover with a damp cloth and keep aside for ten minutes.
4. Add three tablespoons of melted *ghee* and incorporate into the dough gradually. Add almonds, raisins and *chironji*. Knead, cover and keep it in a warm place for thirty minutes to allow the dough to rise.
5. Divide the dough into eight equal sized portions, make balls, cover and keep aside for ten minutes.
6. Preheat the oven to 240°C. Flatten the balls and roll them into a round shape of five inches diameter with a rolling pin. Prick the entire surface with a fork.
7. Arrange the rolled discs on a baking tray and bake it in the preheated oven at 240°C for ten to twelve minutes.
8. Remove from oven, brush *bakarkhani* with *ghee* and serve hot.

Note: There is no need to grease the baking tray as the *Bakarkhanis* will release enough fat while being baked. When you dissolve fresh yeast do not use very hot water, it should be lukewarm.

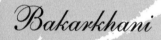

Bakarkhani

Ingredients

For naan

Refined flour (maida)	4 cups
Baking powder	1 tsp
Soda bicarbonate	½ tsp
Salt	to taste
Sugar	2 tsps
Egg	1
Milk	1 cup
Yogurt	2 tbsps
Oil	2 tbsps
Butter	4-6 tsps

For filling

Cottage cheese (paneer)	200 gms
Onions	2 medium sized
Green chillies	2
Fresh coriander leaves	a few sprigs
Fresh mint leaves	a few sprigs
Red chilli powder	½ tbsp
Cumin powder	1 tbsp
Salt	to taste

Method of preparation

1. Sieve flour with baking powder, sodabicarbonate and salt. Add sugar, egg, milk, yogurt and mix. Add water as required and knead into a medium soft dough. Apply one tablespoon of oil, cover with a damp cloth and keep aside for at least an hour.

2. Grate paneer in a bowl and keep aside. Peel, wash and finely chop onions. Remove stems, wash, deseed and finely chop green chillies. Clean, wash and finely chop fresh coriander leaves and mint leaves.

3. In a bowl mix grated paneer, chopped onion, green chillies, coriander and mint leaves, red chilli powder, cumin powder and salt to taste.

4. Divide the paneer mixture into eight equal portions and keep aside.

5. Apply the remaining oil to the dough and knead it again. Divide it into eight equal portions and form them into smooth balls.

6. Preheat oven to 240°C.

7. Flatten a portion of dough, place a portion of the paneer mixture in the centre and fold the dough over to form a ball.

8. Place the stuffed dough on a lightly floured surface and roll gently into a disc of four to five inch diameter.

9. Place on a greased baking tray and bake in the preheated oven at 240°C for about six to eight minutes.

10. Brush the hot kulcha with butter and serve immediately.

Onion Paneer
Kulcha

93

Sheermal

Ingredients

Refined flour (*maida*)	2 cups	Saffron	a few strands
Salt	to taste	Kewra essence	2-3 drops
Sugar	2 tsps	Desi ghee	¼ cup
Milk	¾ cup + 3 tbsps	Butter	2 tbsps + for greasing

Method of preparation

1. Sieve refined flour with salt. Dissolve sugar in three-fourth cup of warm milk and saffron in the remaining three tablespoons of warm milk.
2. Add the dissolved sugar and two to three drops of *kewra* essence to the sieved flour. When fully mixed, add one-eighth cup of water and knead into a soft dough. Cover with a wet muslin cloth and keep aside for ten minutes.
3. Melt *ghee* and add it to the dough and incorporate it well. Knead again into a soft dough. Cover and keep aside for ten minutes.
4. Divide the dough into sixteen equal sized portions and form into balls, cover and keep aside for ten minutes.
5. Preheat the oven to 240° C. Flatten the balls on a lightly floured surface and roll each dough with a rolling pin into round discs of six inch diameter. Prick the entire surface with a fork.
6. Grease a baking tray with butter, arrange the rolled discs on it and bake in the preheated oven for five minutes.
7. Remove, brush the *sheermals* with saffron milk and bake again for three to four minutes.
8. When cooked, remove, brush with butter and serve immediately.

Ingredients

For the roti

Refined flour (maida)................1½ cups
Salt....................................to taste
Oil....................................1 tbsp
Baking powder........................a pinch
Egg....................................1

For the filling

Mutton mince.........................1 cup

Onion..............................1 medium sized
Green chillies.........................2
Fresh coriander leaves.........a few sprigs
Oil.............................2 tbsps + to fry
Salt.................................to taste
Garam masala powder...................¼ tsp
Eggs.................................8

Method of preparation

1. Sieve refined flour and add salt, oil, baking powder and egg. Mix well and knead into a soft dough adding water as required.
2. Divide the dough into eight equal portions and roll into round balls. Keep the dough covered with a damp cloth.
3. Clean and wash mutton mince. Keep in a colander so that all the excess water is drained away. Peel, wash and grate onion. Remove stems, wash and chop green chillies. Clean, wash and chop fresh coriander leaves.
4. Heat two tablespoons of oil in a pan, add grated onion and sauté till light brown. Add mutton mince, green chillies and salt. Cook, covered, on medium heat till the mince is cooked and completely dry. Add garam masala powder and coriander leaves and mix well.
5. Beat the eggs well.
6. Roll out each ball of the dough into a thin square chapati.
7. Place a tablespoon or two of mince in the centre and pour two tablespoons of beaten egg over it. Fold in sides to make a square packet. Heat a non-stick pan and place the chapati packet on it.
8. Pour some more beaten egg over and drizzle oil. Slowly turn over and pour a little more of the beaten egg so that the dough-mince packet is covered with egg on all sides.
9. Gently fry on low heat till all the sides are golden and crisp.
10. Serve hot with green chutney.

Baida Roti

Ingredients

Refined flour (maida)...................4 cups	Fresh coriander leaves..........a few sprigs
Garlic.....................................25 cloves	Sugar..2 tsps
Butter..6 tbsps	Egg..1
Baking powder.............................1 tsp	Milk..1 cup
Soda bicarbonate.........................½ tsp	Yogurt...2 tbsps
Salt...to taste	Oil...2 tbsps

Method of preparation

1. Sieve flour, leaving some aside for dusting, with baking powder, soda bicarbonate and salt. Peel and wash garlic. Grind twenty cloves to a fine paste. Chop the remaining finely. Clean, wash and finely chop coriander leaves.
2. Add sugar, egg, milk, garlic paste, yogurt, chopped garlic, chopped coriander leaves to the flour mixture and mix. Add water as required and knead into a medium soft dough. Apply a little oil, cover with a damp cloth and keep aside for at least an hour.
3. Punch the dough with your hands to make it soft and pliable.
4. Divide the dough into twelve to sixteen equal sized portions, cover and let it rest for an hour more.
5. Melt butter. Flatten each dough ball between your palms, apply melted butter and dust with flour. Roll into a ball again and keep it covered for fifteen minutes.
6. Preheat oven to 250°C.
7. Roll each dough ball on a floured surface into a five to six inch diameter disc. Pull it from one end to get the elongated shape of a *naan*.
8. Cook in the preheated oven at 250°C for seven minutes. You can also cook in a *tandoor* till brown spots appear on the surface. Remove and serve hot drizzled with melted butter.

Note: *Naans can also be cooked on a griddle (tawa) by moistening them on either side with a little water while cooking.*

Butter Garlic Naan

Rajasthani Baati

Ingredients

Whole wheat flour (atta).............2 cups
Baking powder...........................¼ tsp
Salt...2 tsps

Desi ghee...............2/3 cup + for soaking
Carom seeds (ajwain).....................½ tsp

Method of preparation

1. Mix flour, baking powder and salt. Sift and keep aside.
2. Rub two-thirds cup of ghee into the flour mixture till it resembles bread crumbs.
3. Add ajwain and make a dough using three-fourth cup of water.
4. Preheat oven to 220°C.
5. Divide the dough into eight portions and shape them into small balls. Bake them at 220°C for about ten minutes. Lower heat to 200°C and continue to bake for further thirty to thirty-five minutes.
6. Take out, press lightly and soak in a bowl of melted desi ghee for at least one hour.
7. Remove from bowl before serving and serve with dal and ghee.

Chef's tip: Traditionally batis are baked on cow dung cake fire.

(See Photo on Page 102)

Ingredients

Gram flour (besan)......................2 cups	Salt..to taste
Whole wheat flour (atta)...........3/4 cup	Chaat masala..................................1 tsp
Fresh coriander leaves.......1 small bunch	Pomegranate seeds (anardana)......1 tbsp
Green chillies...4	Oil.....................1 tbsp + for greasing
Onion...........................1 medium sized	Butter....................................as required
Turmeric powder............................1 tsp	

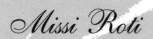

Missi Roti

Method of preparation

1. Clean, wash and chop coriander leaves. Remove stems, wash and chop green chillies. Peel, wash and finely chop onion.
2. Sift together the two flours. Add coriander leaves, green chillies, onion, turmeric powder, salt, *chaat masala*, *anardana* and one tablespoon of oil. Add enough water to form a soft dough. Rest the dough for ten minutes.
3. Divide the dough into sixteen equal sized portions and form into balls.
4. Grease your palms. Grease the tabletop and keep the dough on it. Press a little. Slightly dampen one palm and using both your palms pat the ball between them to make a *chapati* or roll it on a lightly floured surface using a rolling pin to a disc size of six inches diameter.
5. Heat the *tandoor*. Lightly dampen one side of the *chapati* and stick it onto the *tandoor* wall. Alternatively you can roast the *chapati* on a hot *tawa*.
6. Cook till done. Apply butter immediately and serve hot.

(See Photo on Page 102)

Ingredients

Raw jackfruit (kathal)....................½ kg	Yogurt......................................1½ cups
Rice...1½ cups	Oil..to deep fry
Salt...to taste	Desi ghee..................................3 tbsps
Green cardamoms.............................4	Caraway seeds (shahi jeera)............½ tsp
Black cardamoms............................3	Turmeric powder............................1 tsp
Cloves..3	Cumin powder...............................1 tsp
Cinnamon...................2 one inch sticks	Coriander powder.........................2 tsps
Onions...................4 medium sized	Red chilli powder..........................2 tsps
Ginger...............................1½ inch piece	Saffron................................5-6 strands
Garlic..10 cloves	Milk...2 tbsps
Tomatoes.....................3 medium sized	Garam masala powder....................1 tsp
Fresh coriander leaves.......1 small bunch	Kewra water................................1 tbsp
Fresh mint leaves..............1 small bunch	

Method of preparation

1. Apply oil to a knife and cut the jackfruit into slices. Peel and cut into one-and-a-half inch sized cubes. Wash and drain.

2. Pick rice, wash twice and soak in three cups of water for thirty minutes. Drain. Parboil the rice in six cups of water adding a little salt and two green cardamoms, two black cardamoms, cloves and one stick of cinnamon. Drain the parboiled rice, refresh in cold water and drain again.

3. Peel, wash and thinly slice onions. Peel, wash and grind ginger and garlic to a fine paste. Wash and chop tomatoes. Clean, wash and finely chop coriander leaves. Clean, wash and tear mint leaves with hand. Whisk yogurt and keep aside.

4. Heat sufficient oil in a kadai and deep-fry the jackfruit cubes. Drain onto an absorbent paper and keep aside. In the same oil deep-fry half of the onions till golden brown and crisp. Drain onto an absorbent paper and keep aside.

Kathal Ki Biryani

99

5. In another pan heat three tablespoons of *ghee*, add *shahi jeera* and the remaining green cardamoms, black cardamoms, crushed cinnamon. Add the remaining onions and sauté for a while. Add ginger-garlic paste and continue to sauté. Add turmeric powder, cumin powder, coriander powder, red chilli powder, tomatoes and continue to sauté for two to three minutes. Add the fried jackfruit cubes and stir. Add yogurt, salt and coriander leaves.
6. Dissolve the saffron in lukewarm milk and keep aside.
7. Preheat the oven to 200°C.
8. Take a large bowl, arrange half the jackfruit mixture. Over this spread a layer of rice. Sprinkle saffron milk, *garam masala* powder, a few mint leaves and a few drops of *kewra* water. Arrange the rest of the jackfruit mixture. Cover with rice. Garnish with fried onions, remaining mint leaves and the remaining *kewra* water. Cover with aluminium foil and cook in the preheated oven at 200°C for about twenty to twenty-five minutes.
9. Serve hot with a *raita* of your choice.

Ingredients

Refined flour (maida)....................4 cups	Sugar...2½ tsps
Salt..to taste	Desi ghee............¾ cup + to shallow fry
Milk...1 cup	

Varqi Parantha

Method of preparation

1. Sieve flour with salt. Warm milk slightly and dissolve sugar in it.
2. Make a well in the sieved flour, pour the milk and about half cup of water and mix in gradually. When fully mixed, knead to make a soft dough. Cover with a moist cloth and keep aside for ten minutes.
3. Melt *ghee* and add two-thirds of it to the dough, incorporate it gradually and knead it again. Cover and keep aside for ten minutes. Place the dough on a lightly floured surface and flatten with a rolling pin into a rectangular shape.
4. Apply one-fourth of the remaining *ghee* evenly over the rolled dough, dust with flour, fold one end to two-thirds of the rectangle and then fold the other end over it to make three folds. Cover and refrigerate for ten minutes. Repeat this entire process thrice.
5. Remove from the refrigerator and flatten into a rectangle around one-eighth inch thick and make round discs of four inch diameter with a round cutter. Then make three crisscross incisions evenly spaced on the surface of each disc.
6. Place the discs on butter paper sheets and refrigerate until ready to serve.
7. Melt *ghee* on a *tawa* and shallow fry the *paranthas* over low heat until golden brown on both sides. Serve hot.

Chef's tip: The longer you refrigerate the dough, the *paranthas* will become flakier. But do not refrigerate it for more than eight hours.

Ingredients

Green gram (sabut moong)	2 tbsps	Yogurt	2 tbsps
Lentil (sabut masoor)	2 tbsps	Desi ghee	2 tbsps
Black gram (sabut urad)	2 tbsps	Red chilli powder	½ tsp
Bengal gram split (chana dal)	2 tbsps	Turmeric powder	½ tsp
Pigeon pea split (toovar dal)	2 tbsps	Salt	to taste
Onion	1 medium sized	White butter	2 tbsps
Fresh coriander leaves	a few sprigs	Paanch phoran	¼ tsp
Tomatoes	2 medium sized	Garam masala powder	½ tsp

Punj Rattani Dal

Method of preparation

1. Pick and wash grams and dals well. Soak in two cups of water for an hour. Drain and pressure cook with three cups of water till done.
2. Peel, wash and chop onion finely. Clean, wash and chop coriander leaves. Wash and chop tomatoes. Whisk yogurt.
3. Heat *desi ghee* in a thick-bottomed vessel, add onion and fry till it turns a light brown.
4. Add red chilli powder, turmeric powder and stir.
5. Add the cooked *dals* and salt to taste. Mash lightly against the sides of the pan with a ladle. Continue to cook, stirring continuously for two to three minutes.
6. Heat white butter in a deep pan, add *paanch phoron*, chopped tomato, yogurt, *garam masala* powder and sauté on medium heat till fat rises to the surface.
7. Add it to the *dals* and simmer, stirring occasionally for two to three minutes.
8. Serve hot garnished with fresh coriander leaves.

Note: *Paanch phoron* is a mixture of equal quantities of mustard seeds, cumin seeds, fenugreek seeds, fennel seeds and onion seeds.

Ingredients

Black eyed beans (lobia)............1½ cups	Cumin seeds....................................1 tsp
Onions...........................2 medium sized	Fenugreek seeds............................½ tsp
Tomato...........................1 medium sized	Red chillies whole................................2
Fresh coriander leaves.........a few sprigs	Cinnamon...........................1 inch stick
Ginger................................1 inch piece	Turmeric powder...........................½ tsp
Garlic..6 cloves	Red chilli powder.........................2 tsps
Oil...3 tbsps	Salt...to taste

Method of preparation

1. Pick, wash lobia several times. Soak in three cups of water for two hours. Drain and boil in three cups of water until three-fourths cooked. Keep aside along with the cooking liquor.
2. Peel, wash and finely chop onions. Wash and chop tomato. Clean, wash and finely chop coriander leaves. Wash and peel ginger. Peel garlic.
3. In a pan heat one tablespoon of oil and add cumin seeds, fenugreek seeds and red chillies. Sauté for two minutes on low heat stirring constantly till it emits a fragrant aroma. Let cool and grind with ginger and garlic, using a little water, to a smooth paste.
4. Heat the remaining oil in a kadai. Add cinnamon and when it begins to sizzle, add onions. Sauté until lightly browned.
5. Add tomato, ground paste, turmeric powder, red chilli powder and salt. Cover and let it cook in its own juices for five to seven minutes.
6. Add lobia with water. Cover and cook till lobia is tender and gravy almost dry.

Chef's tip: You can serve with scraped fresh coconut.

Lobia Rassedar

Sookhi Urad Dal

Ingredients

Black gram split (dhuli urad dal)...1 cup
Ginger....................................1 inch piece
Green chillies.....................................2
Onions..........................3 medium sized
Tomatoes......................2 medium sized
Oil..4 tbsps
Cloves...4 – 5

Peppercorns.................................10 – 12
Asafoetida...................................a pinch
Red chilli powder...........................½ tsp
Turmeric powder............................½ tsp
Salt...to taste
Garam masala powder..................½ tsp
Lemon juice.................................1 tbsp

Method of preparation

1. Pick and wash dal two-three times. Soak in three cups of water for an hour. Drain and keep aside.
2. Peel, wash and cut ginger into julienne. Remove stems, wash and slit green chillies. Peel, wash and finely slice onions. Wash and chop tomatoes.
3. Boil dal in four cups of water till it is just cooked. Drain water and keep dal aside.
4. Heat two tablespoons of oil in a pan and fry ginger julienne till light brown. Drain and keep aside. In the same oil fry green chillies till they begin to change colour. Drain and keep aside.
5. Add remaining two tablespoons of oil in the same pan and sauté cloves and peppercorns for a minute. Add sliced onions and sauté till golden brown. Add dal, asafoetida, red chilli powder, turmeric powder, salt to taste and stir gently for five minutes. Add chopped tomatoes and sauté for a minute.
6. Sprinkle garam masala powder and lemon juice.
7. Serve garnished with fried ginger julienne and green chillies.

Ingredients

Gram flour (besan)......................¼ cup	Mustard seeds................................½ tsp
Yogurt.......................................2 cups	Cumin seeds..................................½ tsp
Jaggery....................1 lemon sized piece	Red chillies whole................................2
Green chillies..2	Cloves..3 – 4
Curry leaves..............................8 – 10	Cinnamon.........................1 inch stick
Salt..to taste	Asafoetida..................................1/8 tsp
Oil...2 tbsps	

Method of preparation

1. Whisk together besan and yogurt to make a smooth mixture. Add four cups of water and mix well.
2. Grate jaggery. Remove stems, wash and finely chop green chillies. Wash curry leaves and pat them dry.
3. Combine yogurt mixture, jaggery and green chillies.
4. Cook, stirring continuously, till kadhi attains medium consistency. Add salt to taste.
5. Heat oil in a small pan and add mustard seeds, cumin seeds, curry leaves, red chillies, cloves, cinnamon and asafoetida. When seeds begin to crackle, add it to the kadhi and mix well.
6. Serve hot.

Gujarati Kadhi

Ingredients

Bengal gram split (chana dal)........½ cup
Black gram split with skin (chilkewali urad dal).....................................½ cup
Ginger...................................1 inch piece
Green chillies.......................................3
Onion..........................1 medium sized
Tomatoes......................2 medium sized

Fresh coriander leaves...........a few sprigs
Salt...to taste
Turmeric powder............................¼ tsp
Desi ghee...............................2–3 tbsps
Butter...1 tbsp
Cumin seeds...................................1 tsp
Red chilli powder............................½ tsp

Method of preparation

1. Mix the two *dals*, wash and soak in four cups of water for an hour. Drain.
2. Peel, wash and chop ginger finely. Remove stems, wash and chop green chillies. Peel, wash and chop onion finely. Wash and chop tomatoes. Clean, wash and chop coriander leaves.
3. Place soaked *dals* in a pan with four cups of water, salt to taste, turmeric powder, half of the ginger and green chillies. Cover and cook on low heat till the *dals* are tender. Stir well with a ladle to make a homogeneous mixture of the *dals* without mashing them.
4. Heat *desi ghee* and butter in a pan. Add cumin seeds, remaining green chillies and ginger. Stir and add onion and sauté till onion turns light brown.
5. Add tomatoes and sauté till the tomatoes soften. Add red chilli powder and sauté for half a minute.
6. Add the tempering to the *dal* and mix. Simmer for a few minutes and serve hot garnished with chopped coriander leaves.

Maa Chole Di Dal

Ingredients

For pakoras

Gram flour (besan)	¾ cup
Onion	1 medium sized
Fresh fenugreek leaves (methi)	½ small bunch
Ginger	1 inch piece
Carom seeds (ajwain)	1 tsp
Red chilli powder	1 tsp
Baking powder	¼ tsp
Salt	to taste
Oil	to deep fry

For kadhi

Yogurt	1 cup
Gram flour (besan)	¼ cup
Turmeric powder	1 tsp
Salt	to taste
Onion (optional)	1 medium sized
Ginger	½ inch piece
Red chillies whole	2
Oil	2 tbsps
Fenugreek seeds	½ tsp
Cumin seeds	½ tsp
Peppercorns	6
Red chilli powder	1 tsp

Punjabi Kadhi

Method of preparation

1. Peel, wash and chop onion finely. Clean, wash and chop *methi*. Peel, wash and grate ginger. Mix these with the rest of the *pakora* ingredients, except oil, adding about half a cup of water.

2. Heat sufficient oil in a *kadai*, drop small portions of the *besan* mixture and deep fry till golden brown. Drain onto an absorbent paper and keep aside.

3. For *kadhi*, whisk yogurt well and mix *besan*. Blend thoroughly so as to ensure that there are no lumps. Add turmeric powder, salt and three cups of water.

4. Peel, wash and slice onion. Peel, wash and chop ginger. Remove stems and break red chillies into two.

5. Heat oil in a *kadai*. Add fenugreek seeds, cumin seeds, peppercorns and red chillies. Stir-fry for half a minute. Add sliced onions and chopped ginger and stir-fry for a minute. Add yogurt mixture. Bring to a boil and simmer on low heat for about fifteen minutes, stirring occasionally.

6. Add red chilli powder and fried *pakoras* and continue to simmer for four to five minutes.

7. Serve hot with steamed rice.

Rajasthani Dal

Ingredients

Green gram split (moong dal).........½ cup	Turmeric powder..............................1 tsp
Bengal gram split (chana dal)......5 tbsps	Ghee...2 tbsps
Ginger..........................2 one inch pieces	Cumin seeds....................................1 tsp
Onion...........................1 large sized	Asafoetida......................................a pinch
Red chillies whole..............................3	Red chilli powder...........................1 tbsp
Salt..to taste	Dry mango powder (amchur).......1½ tsps

Method of preparation

1. Pick, wash and soak *moong dal* and *chana dal* together in about three cups of water for an hour. Drain. Peel, wash and finely chop ginger and onion. Remove stems and break red chillies into two.

2. Boil dals in four cups of water adding salt to taste, turmeric powder and ginger till cooked.

3. Heat *ghee* in a pan. Add cumin seeds, asafoetida and red chillies to the *ghee* and as cumin seeds begin to change colour, add onion. Cook till onion turns light brown.

4. Add red chilli powder and the cooked *dal* to this. Add half a cup of water and bring to a boil. Reduce heat and simmer for ten minutes. Add *amchur* and stir to mix well.

5. Serve hot with *baati*.

Ingredients

Spinach (palak)..............1 medium bunch	Black gram split (dhuli urad dal)....1 tsp
Onions......................10 small sized	Salt...to taste
Curry leaves.................................2 sprigs	Turmeric powder...........................½ tsp
Pigeon peas split (toovar dal)....1½ cups	Oil...2 tbsps
Coconut......................½ medium sized	Mustard seeds................................1 tsp
Red chillies whole................................5	Asafoetida.......................................¼ tsp
Cumin seeds....................................1 tsp	

Method of preparation

1. Pick, clean, wash and finely chop spinach. Peel and wash onions. Wash curry leaves and pat them dry. Wash toovar dal and soak in three cups of water for half an hour. Drain.
2. Scrape coconut. Remove stems and break red chillies into two. Grind coconut with red chillies, cumin seeds and dhuli urad dal to a fine paste.
3. Pressure cook toovar dal with three cups of water, salt and turmeric powder. Let cool and blend in a liquidizer.
4. Heat oil in a pan and add mustard seeds, curry leaves and asafoetida.
5. When the mustard seeds start to crackle, add coconut paste and fry for three to four minutes.
6. Add onions and spinach and stir-fry for two to three minutes.
7. Add the dal. Mix well and simmer on low heat for ten minutes, stirring occasionally. Adjust seasoning.
8. Serve hot.

Palak
Milakootal

111

Chunda

Ingredients

Raw mangoes............................2 kgs	Sugar...2 kgs
Salt...4 tbsps	Red chilli powder...................2 – 3 tbsps
Turmeric powder.........................½ tsp	Cumin powder...............................2 tsps

Method of preparation

1. Wash, dry, peel and grate the mangoes.
2. Add salt and turmeric powder to the grated mangoes. Mix well and keep aside in a stainless steel or glass vessel for half an hour.
3. Add sugar and mix well.
4. Put the grated mango and sugar in a thick-bottomed vessel. Put the vessel on low heat and cook, stirring constantly.
5. Cook for about thirty to forty minutes or until the water evaporates and a one-string sugar syrup forms. Remove from heat and let it cool.
6. When cooled, add red chilli powder and cumin powder and mix well.
7. Store in a dry, clean, sterilized glass jar with a tight lid.

TIP: Instead of cooking it on direct heat, chunda can be cooked in the heat of sunlight. For that, mix sugar and cover the bowl with a thin cloth or a muslin cloth and leave it in the sun till sugar gets a one string syrup consistency. Then add red chilli powder and cumin powder and keep it again in the sun for a day or two.

Note: Remember to stir it everyday and bring it back into the house at sunset. This quantity of chunda will last a family of four for more than a year.

Ingredients

Dates (khajur)	15–20	Red chilli powder	2 tsps
Cumin seeds	2 tsps	Dry ginger powder (soonth)	1 tsp
Fennel seeds (saunf)	¼ tsp	Black salt	1 tsp
Jaggery (grated)	½ cup	Salt	to taste
Tamarind pulp	1 cup		

Method of preparation

1. Wash, stone dates and chop roughly. Dry roast cumin seeds and fennel seeds. Cool slightly and grind to a powder.
2. Mix together dates, jaggery, tamarind pulp, cumin and fennel powder, red chilli powder, dry ginger powder, black salt, salt to taste and one cup of water. Cook on medium heat till it comes to a boil, reduce heat and continue to cook for six to eight minutes.
3. Cool and serve.

(See Photo on Page 26)

Khajoor Di Chutney

Ingredients

Tomatoes......................8 medium sized	Red chillies whole...............................2
Fresh coriander leaves..........a few sprigs	Jaggery (grated)...........................¼ cup
Oil...2 tbsps	Salt..to taste
Paanch phoron...........................1½ tbsps	

Method of preparation

1. Wash and cut the tomatoes into quarters. Clean, wash and chop coriander leaves.
2. Heat oil in a pan, add *paanch phoron* and whole red chillies. When the seeds start to crackle add tomatoes, two cups of water and cook for ten to fifteen minutes.
3. Add jaggery and salt and cook for another five minutes.
4. Add finely chopped coriander leaves and mix.

Note: *Paanch Phoron* is a mixture of equal quantities of cumin seeds, mustard seeds, fenugreek seeds, fennel seeds and onion seeds.

Tomato Chatni

Bhindi Raita

Ingredients

Ladyfingers (bhindi)................................10-15 medium sized	Salt..to taste
Oil..to deep fry	Red chilli powder.....................1 ½ tsps
Yogurt..4 cups	Cumin powder...............................1 tsp

Method of preparation

1. Wash, wipe dry, remove head and tail and slice *bhindis* diagonally.
2. Heat sufficient oil in a *kadai* and deep fry *bhindis* till crisp. Drain onto an absorbent paper.
3. Whisk together yogurt, salt, red chilli powder and cumin powder. Chill in the refrigerator for half an hour.
4. Add three-fourth of the fried *bhindis* to the yogurt mixture just before serving. Mix. Garnish with the remaining fried *bhindis* and serve immediately.

Ingredients

Refined flour (maida)................1½ cups   Yogurt..8 tbsps
Sodabicarbonate............................¼ tsp   Sugar..2 cups
Pistachios..4-5   Milk..2 tbsps
Ghee......................2/3 cup + to deep fry

Method of preparation

1. Sieve flour and sodabicarbonate together. Finely chop pistachios.
2. Rub in two-thirds cup of ghee into the flour mixture till it resembles breadcrumbs.
3. Add beaten yogurt and knead into a soft dough. Cover and allow it to stand for forty-five minutes.
4. Divide into twelve equal portions and shape into smooth balls. Take care not to overwork the dough.
5. Make a slight dent in the centre of the ball with your thumb. Keep the balls covered.
6. Heat sufficient ghee in a kadai and when it is medium hot, add the prepared dough balls and deep fry on very slow heat. If necessary you may place a tava below the kadai so that the oil does not get too hot.
7. Gradually the balushahis will start floating to the top. Turn gently and fry on the other side till golden. The entire process may take around half an hour to forty-five minutes.
8. Drain and allow to cool to room temperature. This can be an overnight process.
9. Heat together sugar and one cup of water till it reaches a two-string consistency. Midway through add milk to the cooking syrup so that the scum rises to the surface. Carefully remove this scrum and throw away.
10. Remove the syrup from heat and soak the fried balushahis in it for thirty minutes.
11. Gently remove the balushahis from the sugar syrup and place on a serving plate. Garnish with chopped pistachios. Serve when the sugar has hardened.

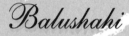

Balushahi

Kaju Katli

Ingredients

Cashewnut powder	3 ½ cups	Liquid glucose	2 tbsps
Sugar	1 1/3 cups	Ghee	1½ tbsps
Water	1 1/3 cups	Silver warq	as required

Method of preparation

1. Cook sugar and water together till the syrup reaches 118°C and you get multi strings. Then add liquid glucose and ghee and stir well.
2. Remove from heat and add cashewnut powder stirring continuously. If necessary add one tablespoon of water and keep stirring till the temperature comes down to 65°C.
3. Knead lightly to make a soft dough. Roll out on a flat greased surface to one centimetre thickness.
4. Rub a butter paper over the surface to smoothen it evenly. Apply silver warq and cut into diamond shapes. Store in an airtight container.

(See Photo on Page 119)

Ingredients

Khoya/mawa	500 gms	Milk	3 tbsps
Walnut kernels	½ cup	Oil	for greasing
Sugar	½ cup	Dark chocolate	300 gms

Method of preparation

1. Grate khoya into a bowl and keep aside. Roughly chop walnuts, keep a few aside for garnishing.
2. Heat a pan, add grated khoya and roast for four to five minutes.
3. Add sugar, chopped walnuts and milk and cook till it thickens.
4. Melt dark chocolate in a double boiler. Pass it through a sieve if there are any lumps. Bring melted chocolate to room temperature.
5. Divide the cooked khoya mixture into three equal parts. To one part add one-third of the melted chocolate. Mix well.
6. Grease a tray with oil. Pour one part of plain khoya mixture onto it and spread evenly. Shake the tray so that mixture spreads evenly. Now spread the chocolate khoya mixture over and finally top with the remaining plain khoya mixture. Let it cool for forty-five minutes to one hour. When completely cooled, cut into square or diamond shaped pieces and keep.
7. Holding the burfi pieces by their edges dip into the remaining melted chocolate so that only the top side of the burfi is covered with the melted chocolate. Garnish with walnut pieces and keep it in the refrigerator for thirty minutes before serving.

Note: A double boiler contains of two pots, one which sits on top of the other. The bottom pot contains boiling water, the top pot contains whatever is being cooked. This tool is useful for making delicate sauces or melting chocolate or any other occasion when you don't want to have direct heat on the food which is being cooked. You can improvise a double boiler by placing the items to be cooked in a metal bowl, which is placed over a pot of boiling water.

Chocolate Walnut Burfi

Ingredients

Khoya/mawa.............................1½ cups	Sugar...2 cups
Chenna.......................................¼ cup	Lemon juice...................................½ tsp
Soda bi carbonate.........................¼ tsp	**Stuffing**
Refined flour (maida)................3 tbsps	Pistachios...6
Green cardamom powder...............¼ tsp	Gulkand.....................................3 tbsps
Ghee/oil...............................to deep fry	

Method of preparation

1. Grate khoya and mash chenna. Mix the two with sodabicarbonate, refined flour, green cardamom powder and a little water to make a soft dough. Divide into sixteen equal portions.

2. Chop pistachios and mix with gulkand. Stuff each portion of the khoya-chenna ball with a little of this mixture and shape into balls.

3. Prepare a thin syrup with sugar and equal quantity of water. Add lemon juice to the sugar syrup and when the scum rises to the surface, gently remove it.

4. Heat sufficient ghee/oil in a kadai. Add the balls and deep fry on very low heat till golden in colour.

5. Drain and soak in the sugar syrup for atleast fifteen to twenty minutes before serving.

Chef's tip : Temperature of the ghee/oil should be low while frying the gulab jamuns as otherwise they will remain uncooked from inside.

Gulab
-e-
Gulkand

Ingredients

Milk	7½ cups	Ghee	2 tbsps
Vermicelli	100 gms	Green cardamom powder	¼ tsp
Almonds	8-10	Nutmeg powder	a pinch
Pistachios	8-10	Sunflower seeds (chironji)	2 tbsps
Saffron	a few strands	Sugar	½ cup

Sheer Kurma

Method of preparation

1. Blanch almonds and pistachios in hot water. Drain, peel and cut into slivers. Soak saffron in two tablespoons of warm milk.
2. Heat ghee in a thick bottomed vessel. Add vermicelli and sauté for three to four minutes or till light golden. Add milk and bring to a boil. Reduce heat and simmer till the milk thickens and turns light pink in colour.
3. Add cardamom powder, nutmeg powder, saffron, sunflower seeds, almonds, pistachios and sugar and continue to simmer for another ten minutes.
4. Serve hot.

(For Photo see Page 120)

Ingredients

Milk	12 cups	Saffron	10–12 strands
Vinegar	2 tbsps	Rose water	1 tbsp
Cornstarch	2 tsps	Sugar	2 cups
Green cardamom powder	1 tsp	Refined flour (maida)	2 tbsps
Pistachios	8–10		

Method of preparation

1. Boil seven cups of milk. Once it comes to a boil take off the heat. After cooling for seven to eight minutes add vinegar and let the milk curdle. Do not stir at this moment.

2. Strain and tie up the solids in a muslin cloth and hang it up so that the excess water is drained away.

3. Transfer the solids onto a flat surface while still warm and start kneading it with the palm of your hand. Add cornstarch and continue to knead till you get a soft dough. Cover and keep aside.

4. Heat the remaining milk and once it comes to a boil, lower the heat and let it simmer till it is reduced to a thick creamy consistency. Add green cardamom powder and mix.

5. Chop the pistachios for garnish. Dissolve saffron in rose water and keep aside.

6. Make a syrup with sugar and two cups of water and keep it on simmer.

7. Divide the dough into ten to twelve equal sized balls and shape into ovals. Gently lower these ovals into the simmering syrup.

8. Once the ovals rise to the top, sprinkle some cold water and a little flour and continue to simmer. Again sprinkle some cold water and a little flour when the ovals rise to the top. Repeat this a couple of times more.

9. Drain the ovals and arrange them on a plate. When they have cooled spread the thickened milk on the surface of each oval. Sprinkle the chopped pistachios and the saffron dissolved in rose water.

10. Serve at room temperature.

Ingredients

Whole wheat flour (atta)...........2 cups	Almonds...10
Semolina (sooji)..........................4 tbsps	Raisins...10
Ghee....................1½ cups + to deep fry	Powdered sugar............................¾ cup
Milk.....................................as required	Green cardamom powder...............¼ tsp
Cashewnuts.......................................10	

Choorma Laddoo

Method of preparation

1. Mix flour and semolina in a bowl. Add half a cup of melted ghee and mix well. Add milk as required and knead into a stiff dough.
2. Divide the dough into lemon sized balls.
3. Heat sufficient ghee in a kadai and deep-fry the balls on medium heat, till they are well done. Drain onto an absorbent paper and cool.
4. Coarsely grind the wheat balls in a mixer. Chop cashewnuts and almonds. Wash raisins and pat them dry.
5. Add powdered sugar, cardamom powder, cashewnuts, almonds, raisins and one cup of warm ghee to the coarsely powdered wheat balls.
6. Mix well and form into laddoos while it is still warm. Cool and store in an airtight container.

Ingredients

Gram flour (besan)........................4 cups	Desi ghee................2 cups + for greasing
Pistachios......................................10–12	Green cardamom powder................½ tsp
Almonds..10–12	Sugar (powdered)..........................2 cups

Method of preparation

1. Cut the pistachios and almonds into thin slivers.
2. Heat *ghee* in a *kadai*, add the *besan* and roast it on low heat stirring continuously for ten to fifteen minutes or till it starts changing colour and gives out a nice aroma.
3. Add cardamom powder, almonds and pistachio slivers and mix. Remove from heat and let it cool.
4. Add the powdered sugar and mix well.
5. Grease a tray with *ghee*. Pour the *besan* mixture and spread it evenly on the tray.
6. Let it cool and then cut into square and diamond shaped pieces and serve. While storing keep in an airtight container.

Besan Burfi

Kesar Pista Kulfi with Falooda

Ingredients

Pistachios.................................15-20

Milk.............................6 cups + 2 tbsps

Cornstarch..................................½ tbsp

Sugar...1 cup

Khoya/mawa (grated)..................5 tbsps

Or

Thick fresh cream.........................½ cup

Saffron...........................a few strands

Rose/khus syrup..........................2 tbsps

For Falooda

Cornstarch..................................½ cup

Saffron...............................few strands

Method of preparation

1. To make *falooda*, mix two cups of water and cornstarch together. Soak saffron strands in warm water and puree it using a small pestle.
2. Cook cornstarch mixture on low heat, stirring all the time ,till the mixture becomes thick and gelatinous. Add the pureed saffron and mix well.
3. Transfer the mixture to a *falooda* press, and press in continuous stream into a bowl of chilled water. Drain the water and store the *falooda* strands for serving with *kulfi*.
4. Blanch the pistachios and slice thinly.
5. Boil milk till it is reduced to two cups. Add cornstarch dissolved in two tablespoons of cold milk and cook till the consistency is like that of a thick sauce.
2. Add sugar and stir till completely dissolved. Remove from heat and add crushed *khoya* or thick cream, pistachios and saffron. Cool.
3. Fill the *kulfi* moulds with the mixture and screw the tops securely. If *kulfi* moulds are not available, use ice-trays.
4. Place the moulds on their side, in the deep-freeze compartment of the refrigerator and freeze for three to four hours.
5. Before serving, dip each mould in warm water, unscrew top and turn onto a bed of *falooda*.
6. Drizzle some rose syrup or khus syrup on top.

Note: Ready *falooda* is easily available in the market.

Coconut Milk : Grate coconut. Put it in a blender. For each cup of grated coconut, use one-fourth cup of water and blend it properly. Pass it through a strainer pressing firmly to extract all the juice (first milk). This process can be repeated to get the second, thinner milk from the same solids.

Ginger Paste : Take a two-inch sized piece of ginger, scrape, wash and cut into small pieces. Put it in a mixer, add two tablespoons of water and make a smooth paste. Store refrigerated.

Garlic Paste : Take fifteen to twenty cloves of garlic. Peel, wash and put in a mixer with two tablespoons of water. Make a smooth paste and use as required. Store refrigerated.

Cashewnut Paste : Soak 250 gms of cashewnuts in two cups of water for half an hour. Drain, put it in a mixer with half a cup of water and grind to a smooth paste. Store refrigerated.

Onion Paste : Peel, wash and cut onion into quarters. Put in a mixer and make a paste without adding any water. Store refrigerated.

Tamarind Pulp : Soak 100 gms of tamarind in half a cup of lukewarm water for half an hour. Force the soaked tamarind through a strainer and obtain the pulp.

Deep Frying : The food is completely immersed in hot fat/oil and cooked. In most cases, deep frying ensures cooking with colouring of exteriors. Deep frying is done at a temperature of 150-180°C/300-350°F. For e.g Gulab jamun, vada, etc.

Glossary

Tadka :	On completing some preparations like *dal*, a mixture of spices and/or herbs are fried in hot *ghee* or oil or butter and then added. This process is also known as tempering.
Roasting :	It is a dry method of cooking (i.e. without addition of moisture). A small quantity of fat/oil/butter is taken and the item to be roasted is put in/with that and cooked till the required result is obtained. Roasting can be done in a pan or in an oven/tandoor.
Dum :	Cooking a dish on slow heat, covered and sealed, for a long duration is known as *dum* style of cooking.
Dhuan :	The dish is cooked/given flavour by smoke generated from a source which can be live coals or burning wood dust. For giving smoky flavour to "Baingan Ka Bhartha" take mashed, roasted brinjal, place it in a flat dish, take a live hot coal in a *katori* (bowl), place it in the centre, pour a tablespoon of hot *ghee* or oil on it, cover immediately and keep for three to four minutes. Some flavourings like cloves/cardamom too can be added in the *katori*.
Sprouted Moong :	Take whole *moong* (green gram) and soak it overnight. Remove excess water and tie it in a muslin or cotton cloth, keep for eight to nine hours in a warm and dark place preferably sprinkling water on it occasionally.
Boiled Onion Paste :	Take sliced onions, add sufficient water to just cover it, add some whole *garam masala* such as green cardamom, black cardamom, cinnamon and cook together till onions become translucent and excess water evaporates. Discard whole *garam masala* and

	grind onions to a fine paste. This is used in making traditional white gravies.
Brown Onion Paste :	Take sliced onions and deep fry in hot oil till its golden brown in colour. Remove onto an absorbent paper, allow it to cool. Grind to a fine paste with yogurt. This is used in traditional Awadhi and Hyderabadi recipes.
Blanching :	Putting vegetables in boiling water for a short duration of time and then refreshing in cold water to remove skin, dirt and also to brighten the colour is called blanching.
Boiling :	To cook food in water or stock when the temperature of water or stock is 100°C is called boiling.
Chopping :	Reducing food into smallest sized pieces by cutting is called chopping.
Dicing :	To cut food into perfect cubes of various sizes is called dice.
Julienne :	Cutting of vegetable into slices first and then further cutting them into fine strips is known as julienne.
Shredding :	To cut leafy vegetables e.g. Spinach, Cabbage. into thin long strips is called shredding.
De-veining :	To remove the center vein from the prawn or lobster before cooking is de-veining. Shell has to be removed, an incision is to be given on the top horizontally to locate the vein.
Filleting :	Fish pieces obtained after de-boning and removing skin (optional) using a sharp knife is filleting.
Shallow Frying :	Food cooked in pan with little fat/oil so that only bottom and side surfaces of the food are immersed is

called shallow frying. This method ensures excellent colour and crispness to the fried product. e.g patties, cutlets, etc.

Parboiling : Cooking to a certain extent only by boiling or simmering is par boiling.

Marinating : Covering the food item, usually meats, with oil, tenderisers, spices, seasonings etc. to tenderise is called marinating. It also gives good taste and facilitates fast cooking.

Poaching : Poaching is cooking slowly in liquid at low temperature around 80 °C and not allowing the liquid to boil. It is a special technique to cook delicate food products e.g poaching eggs, fish etc.

Pureeing : A smooth mixture obtained by grinding cooked vegetables to a smooth paste and passing through a sieve/strainer if required.

Sautéing : To cook vegetables or meat in a shallow pan in a small quantity of cooking medium without much stirring.

Searing : Cooking of meat at a high temperature in some cooking medium to seal the outer part so that the meat remains moist and soft from inside and does not become dry.

Simmering : To cook food gently in water, stock or any other liquid medium that bubbles steadily just below boiling point so that the food cooks in even heat without breaking up.

Whisking : To blend certain food material using a whisker or fork so that you get a smooth consistency. E.g. egg, yogurt.

Subscribe to the most acclaimed food site
www.sanjeevkapoor.com **and avail of unbelievable offers!!!**

Pay **Rs.600*** only for one year subscription instead of normal subscription charges of **Rs. 1000/-** and get Sanjeev Kapoor Books worth **Rs. 750/- FREE** (only upto 31ˢᵗ July, 2003).

You will also have access to more than 1000 recipes other than those published in his books besides many other sections, which will be a rare culinary treat to any food lover. In addition to online contests, etc. you will also have opportunities to win fabulous prizes.

Sanjeev Kapoor also invites all food lovers to participate in the Khana Khazana Quiz and win BIG prizes every week. Watch *Khana Khazana* on Zee TV, answer one simple question based on that day's episode correctly, combine it with a favourite recipe of yours and you can be the lucky winner going places.

*Add Service tax Rs. 48.00

Normal Subscription	You Pay	Plus You Get	You Save
Rs 1,000.	Rs 600 (add service tax Rs. 48/-)	Sanjeev Kapoor's books worth **Rs 750 free.**	Rs 1,150.

*Offer open only up to July 31ˢᵗ, 2003

**Delivery address for free books must be in India.

The three books free with each subscription are

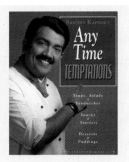

☐ Yes, I would like to subscribe to **www.sanjeevkapoor.com** for one year.

Great Offer from the Khazana of Master Chef Sanjeev Kapoor.

Take your pick of book/books and avail of fantastic discounts.

Number of books	You save
1	Rs.25
2	Rs.100
More than two	Rs.200

Please tick the boxes below to indicate the books you wish to purchase.

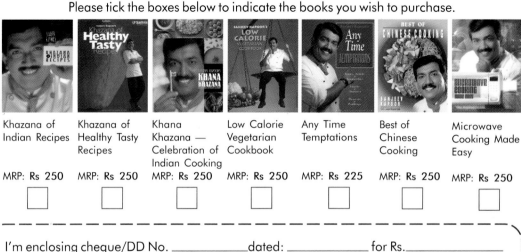

Khazana of Indian Recipes	Khazana of Healthy Tasty Recipes	Khana Khazana — Celebration of Indian Cooking	Low Calorie Vegetarian Cookbook	Any Time Temptations	Best of Chinese Cooking	Microwave Cooking Made Easy
MRP: Rs 250	MRP: Rs 250	MRP: Rs 250	MRP: Rs 250	MRP: Rs 225	MRP: Rs 250	MRP: Rs 250
☐	☐	☐	☐	☐	☐	☐

I'm enclosing cheque/DD No. _____ dated: _____ for Rs. _____

(Rupees in words): _____ only drawn

on (specify bank and branch) _____

favouring **Popular Prakashan Pvt Ltd, Mumbai**

Name: Mr./Ms _____

Address: _____

_____

City: _____ Pin: _____ State: _____

Phone Res: _____ Off: _____ E-mail: _____

Please fill in the coupon in capital letters and mail it with your cheque/DD to :

Popular Prakashan Pvt Ltd,
35-C, Pt Madan Mohan Malaviya Marg, Tardeo, Mumbai – 400 034.
Phone: 022-24941656,24944295 Fax: 022-24945294,
E-mail: info@popularprakashan.com